The Wildest

Dreams of Kew

A PROFILE OF NEPAL

BY
JEREMY BERNSTEIN

PHOTOGRAPHS BY CLAUDE JACCOUX

SIMON AND SCHUSTER · NEW YORK

First printing

SBN 671–20498–X
Library of Congress Catalog Card Number: 71–101865
Designed by Edith Fowler
Manufactured in the United States of America
by American Book–Stratford Press, Inc.

Parts of this book were published originally in The New Yorker

Acknowledgments

I owe a debt of gratitude to a great many people both for making our trip to Nepal possible and for helping me to gather the material presented in this book. In the former category, that our trip was possible at all is thanks to the editor of *The New Yorker*, William Shawn. Mr. Shawn encouraged us to make the trip and came to our rescue in financing it. Without the help of *The New Yorker* we simply would not have gotten to Nepal. In preparing the material for *The New Yorker* articles, which were based on the book, and in helping to edit the book itself I was very much aided by Gardner Botsford of *The New Yorker* editorial staff. I have been guided in my choice of material by his advice throughout. We are also indebted to Stanley Kubrick for some sage advice on photography. One of Kubrick's dicta was that one can never have too many light meters. Both of the ones that we *did* have broke while we were in the Nepalese back country, and it was only Jaccoux's expertise in mountain photography that saved us from a complete photographic catastrophe.

I spent a considerable amount of time with most of the people quoted in the book, and I am grateful collectively to them all and especially to Boris Lissanevitch, and his family, at the Hotel Royal. Boris took us under his generous wing and helped us to meet most of the people that we met in Kathmandu. There were, in addition to Boris, several people who have been enormously helpful to us, and who are not mentioned in the text. This is the place to thank them. In the first instance there is Elizabeth Ann Hawley, who, besides functioning as the *éminence grise* of the Tiger Tops Hotel, is also the Time-Life and Reuters correspondent in Nepal. Elizabeth knows as much about that fascinating country as anyone can know and she was, for us, a gold mine of information, both while we were there and by letter after we left. I am also grateful to Barbara Adams, another knowledgeable member of the American colony in Kathmandu, for her help and hospitality. I am also happy to thank Dr. John McKinnon and his wife, Diane, for their kindness when we visited their hospital in Khumjung, high up in the Sherpa country. Dr. Ray Fort of the United States AID mission in Kathmandu spent several days with me showing me how the AID program functions in Nepal. He also checked my manuscript for accuracy. I am very grateful to Ambassador Carol Laise for her help when we were in Nepal and for reading the manuscript of the articles, and for the kindness of the staff of the American Embassy in Kathmandu and especially Gene Boster, who gave us every possible cooperation.

To these and the rest of the people, Nepalese and non-Nepalese, who made our trip such a rewarding experience, *namaste*—greetings—and many thanks.

JEREMY BERNSTEIN

Contents

Acknowledgments • 7

1 • The Jewel and the Lotus • 13

2 • Fortune Has Wings • 53

3 • Some Walk-Going • 129

4 • L'Envoi • 169

Selected Bibliography • 177

Index • 179

A picture section follows page 96.

Still the world is wondrous large—
    Seven Seas from marge to marge—
And it holds a vast of various kinds of man;
And the wildest dreams of Kew
    are the facts of Kathmandu
And the crimes of Clapham
    chaste at Martaban.
                                —RUDYARD KIPLING

1
The Jewel and the Lotus

*O*nce upon a time there was a lake called the Serpent's Lake, for Karkotak, the king of the serpents, dwelt in it. It was a big, beautiful lake surrounded by lofty mountains. All water plants except the lotus grew in it, and one day Vipaswi Buddha came and threw a root of the lotus into the water.

"When this root shall produce a flower," declared the Buddha, "then Shoyambhu, the Self-Existent One, shall be revealed here in the form of a flame. Then the water in this lake shall go and there shall be a valley wherein shall flourish many towns and villages."

Years passed.

Lotus leaves were seen floating upon the water. And then the predicted flower bloomed in all its heavenly beauty, with a flame of five colors playing upon it.

Knowing that the Self-Existent One had been revealed in the lake, another Buddha, the Sikhi, made a pilgrimage to it with a large number of his followers. He went round the Serpent's Lake thrice and sat down to meditate at the top of a mountain; then he called his disciples together and told them of the future of the holy lake. He also informed them that it was time for him to leave the world, and amidst the lamentation of the men the Sikhi Buddha plunged into the lake and was absorbed in the spirit of the Self-Existent One.

Another long period elapsed, and the Visambhu Buddha arrived at the lake. Like his predecessors, he was accompanied by numerous followers to the Self-Existent One, and then he declared to his retinue, "The Bodhisattva shall duly arrive here and let the water out of the lake." With that, the Buddha departed.

About this time in north China, the Bodhisattva Manjusri was meditating upon world events. When he knew that the Self-Existent One had been revealed in the Serpent's Lake, he called his followers, among whom was a person of high rank named Dharmarkar, and he set out, accompanied by them, for the holy lake.

Arriving at the lake, Manjusri went around it until he came to a low hill in the south. Then he drew his scimitar and cut a passage through the hill, and the water gushed out. The Bodhisattva then told his followers to settle down in the newly formed valley, and he departed, leaving Dharmarkar to become Nepal's first ruler.

This is the legend of the origin of the Kathmandu Valley. It is as close to an historical account of ancient Nepal as is available (archeology is, even now, in its infancy in the country), and like many Nepalese legends, there is a good deal about it that is true. Until about seventy million years ago, according to the geologists, the Indian and Asiatic continents were separated by a sea, the Himalayan Sea, located about where the Himalayan chain is now. The Asiatic continent drifted south, and when it collided with the Indian continent the soft alluvial sea bottom was squeezed up. Gradually the Himalayan Sea was divided by the rising mountains into what are known as the Tibetan Sea, now a high desertic plain north of the mountains, and the Gangeatic Sea, now the flat plain of north India, to the south. In the middle was left a fantastic land of high mountains, deep gorges and lakes. The Kathmandu Valley, which lies slightly to the east of the middle of modern Nepal, was, as is shown by fossils as well as by the alluvial character of the rich soil in the valley, such a lake. (The only sizable lakes now left in Nepal are in the midwestern region of the country, near Pokhara, at the foothills of Annapurna.) The place near Kathmandu where Manjusri cut the mountains with his scimitar to liberate the waters is well known to every Nepali. It is the Chobar Gorge, three miles south of the city of Kathmandu. It is a remarkably sharp gorge, through which the sacred Bagamati River flows southward into the Ganges. The gorge is spanned by a steel suspension bridge with a wooden plank flooring; and despite the fact that this is the oldest steel bridge in the country, dating back about a half century, and that it sways and creaks when one walks over it, it is one of the better footbridges in Nepal.

The Kathmandu Valley floor ranges in altitude between four thousand and five thousand feet. The country as a whole exhibits the widest altitude variation of any country on earth—from 150 feet above sea level in the south near India to 29,028 feet at the summit of Mount Everest, which lies on the border between Tibet and Nepal in the north. Since Nepal is at about the latitude of Florida, the country is tropical wherever the altitude is low. In a general sort of way the average altitude increases as one goes from the south to the Himalayas on the northern frontier. The width of Nepal varies from ninety to 150 miles; it is, as a whole, a rectangularly shaped country bounded by India on the west and Sikkim on the east, with the long side of the rectangle stretching about five hundred miles.

The south of Nepal is a flat region—an extension of the Gangeatic plain—known as the Terai. It varies between five and fifty-five miles in width and consists of rice paddies, forests and jungles. (The Terai jungle has been one of the most famous big-game hunting grounds in the world and still contains its share of tigers, cobras and pythons, crocodiles and the one-horned Asian rhinoceros, whose horn, when ground up, produces a powder that is sold abroad as an aphrodisiac.) After the lower forests, the Himalayan foothills, which rise ten thousand feet or more, begin and extend up to the main Himalayan chain in the north. This part of the country is ribbed by gigantic gorges that have been created by the rivers running southward from the Himalayas. The geological forces that produced the mountains have twisted the rivers and the gorges and have left an occasional large valley—a former lake. The Kathmandu Valley, which has a population of about a half-million people (the total population of the country, which grows at a rate of somewhere between two and three percent a year, is now about eleven million), is the largest valley. It is circular in shape and has an area of 218 square miles. Since the valley is neither very high nor very low, it has rather temperate weather, with temperatures that never exceed ninety degrees in the hot months of May and June and never get much below thirty-six degrees in the coldest month, January. Even in the winter months the sun warms the air during the day, it almost never snows, and it is rarely necessary to put on a sweater before evening.

Throughout the history of the country the Kathmandu Valley has been the cultural and political locus of Nepal. In fact, until the last twenty years internal communication was so bad among the different communities in Nepal that a large fraction of the population was hardly aware that it belonged to any sort of nation at all. For most people in the hills or the Terai, "Nepal" meant the Kathmandu Valley, and in 1958 King Mahendra Bir Bikram Shah Deva, the present ruler of Nepal, in an attempt to stimulate a national conscience, issued a decree asking the population to refrain from using "Nepal" in reference to the valley alone.

It is simply not known who the original settlers of the valley were. It is believed that the aboriginal population was overrun and absorbed during a series of migrations into the valley, ending in the seventh century B.C., by an Indo-Mongoloid race known as the Kirantis, from whom the present occupants of the valley evolved. In 536 B.C. the Gautama Buddha was born in the village of Lumbini in what is now the southern part of Nepal—the Terai. Legend has it that the Buddha visited the Kathmandu Valley. According to one account, he and his party were warned before leaving, "In Nepal the ground is nothing but rocks, and it is as humpy as the back of a camel. Surely you are not going to enjoy your journey." Whether because of the Buddha's visit or otherwise, the Kirantis became Buddhists, and by the third century B.C. some of the most famous Buddhist shrines in the valley —the stupas at Swayambhunath, a hill near Kathmandu where the first lotus took root and flowered, and at Bodnath, a small town a few miles northeast of Kathmandu—had been built. A stupa is a representation of the contemplating Buddha. In form it has a hemispherical bottom, the *garbh*, representing Buddha's body. At the top of the hemisphere is a cube—Buddha's face. All the faces of the cube are painted to show the Buddha's eyes. His nose is often represented by a curious figure like a question mark that is usually interpreted as the Sanskrit symbol for "one"—as in the "oneness" or "uniqueness" of Buddha. In the middle of each of the four foreheads there is a third eye. In Bodnath the four middle eyes have been fitted with electric-light bulbs which give the stupa an uncanny appearance when viewed at night. During the day the outstanding feature of the stupas is the eyes, which, as one writer has remarked, have "a fascinating aspect of mingled meditation and detached watchfulness." They seem to follow you as you go around the base. Above the face is a series of coils, sometimes in metal and sometimes in stone, that represent Buddha's hair. The legend has it that the Buddha was meditating one day when it occurred to him that he was losing a certain amount of time away from his contemplation by the necessity of getting periodic haircuts. At once, the story says, his hair became tightly coiled and turned blue, and no further haircuts were required. In the countryside, especially in the north, near Tibet, the landscape is dotted with stupas, many of which have, through age and neglect, lost their eyes but still retain a haunting suggestion of the original face.

The community of Bodnath is built in a circle surrounding the central stupa. It has long been a place of pilgrimage for Buddhists, especially from Tibet. Since the Chinese takeover of Tibet in the 1950s a certain number of Tibetan refugees have settled in Bodnath—there are about eight thousand Tibetan refugees left in Nepal out of the original group of fifteen thousand or so, the rest having re-migrated to India to join the Dalai Lama, spiritual leader of the Lamaistic Buddhists—and they ply their traditional trades such as farming and rug weaving. The Tibetans are extraordinarily persuasive salesmen, and any visitor to Nepal almost inevitably comes away with Tibetan statuary and *thankas*, religious wall scrolls, which, he is assured, were brought down from the *ghompas*—monasteries—in Lhasa. There is a thriving industry in the valley which is engaged in manufacturing imitation ancient Tibetan monastery art, and it may be just as well for the visitor that it is now all but impossible to find the real thing, since it is against the law in Nepal to export anything that is more than a hundred years old.

In Bodnath there is a man of Nepalese origin who claims to be the Dalai Lama's "representative" in Nepal—the so-called "Chini Lama," Chinese Lama. Having met a few lamas and most especially the reincarnated head lama of the monastery in Thyangboche—a few miles from Mount Everest—and having been enormously impressed by the spiritual and human qualities of the ones that I had met, I looked forward to meeting the Chini Lama on my first visit to Bodnath. I was somewhat shaken when the driver of the car that took me to Bodnath allowed that the Chini Lama had for sale a particularly fine collection of Tibetan rugs. The lama, a middle-aged man, lives in a small but elegant stone dwelling near the stupa. One climbs a wooden staircase to his quarters and removes one's shoes before entering the great man's presence. His living room looked like a museum or the display room of an art gallery. When I walked in, there were several people with the lama, two of whom turned out to be art dealers from India. The lama himself is a spherical figure, shaped something like the stupa, which one can contemplate from his window. Unlike the Buddha, the Chini Lama has a totally bald round head. He motioned for me to sit down on a rug and, while drinking his morning tea, proceeded to study me with curiosity. After a few minutes of total silence, he held out an incredible statue, gold-plated, with dozens of arms, each arm holding a perfectly formed tiny gilded bird. His first words were, in English, "I'll bet that you have never seen one like this. It is worth fifteen hundred U.S. dollars." When it became clear that I was not going to buy his statue the lama lost interest in me and returned to bargaining with the art dealers. After inspecting a few rugs, I left. Later I was told that the Chini Lama also runs the only Tibetan distillery in the valley. He is completely untypical of the Buddhist religious leaders that I met, and the people in the Kathmandu Valley don't have a great deal of use for him.

The main Buddhist sanctuary in the valley is Swayambhunath, situated on the top of a wooded hill just west of Kathmandu. It is best approached by climbing the three hundred steps that lead, rather steeply, to the summit. One first encounters a row of three very large, striking, and rather cruel-looking Buddhas that have been painted in bright colors. Everywhere one looks there are small brown monkeys. (The monkey, like the cow, is a sacred, protected animal in Nepal, but this does not seem to stop the children who play near Swayambhunath from taking an occasional shot at them with small slingshots.) On the top of the hill there is a large cleared plateau every square foot of which contains religious monuments. There is a huge stupa and dozens of small stupas; there is a large metal *dorje* (a symbolic lightning bolt); there are rows of prayer wheels that have "*Om mani padme hum"*—a sacred religious formula sometimes translated to mean "The jewel is in the lotus" or "Hail to the jewel and the lotus"—engraved on the sides. The wheel, the wheel of life, representing the endless cycle of birth and rebirth, is one of the most important Buddhist symbols. To turn a prayer wheel adds to one's *sönam*—a measure of credit which a Buddhist hopes to accumulate in his present life in order to escape the pain of rebirth. In the mountainous countryside of Nepal, where the wheel for transportation is unknown, the only wheels one ever sees are wooden carousels that the Nepalis have constructed for their children to play on, water wheels for grinding corn or millet, prayer wheels and potters' wheels. In the high mountain country near Tibet, one encounters prayer wheels that are turned by water in a stream; a bell rings each time a cycle is completed, and with the rushing stream it makes a lovely sound.

At the top of the hill one encounters a cross section from among all the races of Nepal: Sherpas and Tibetans from the north; Newars, the racial group that succeeded the Kirantis, in the valley; Gurungs, Magars, Sunwars, Rais and Limbus—the hill peoples from whom the Ghurka soldiers are recruited; and a few Tharus, who have come north from the Terai to visit Kathmandu. (There are at least thirty separate local languages in Nepal and at least that many tribal groups. The official language of the country is Nepali, an Indo-Aryan language, derived from Sanskrit, which most of the population can now speak or understand. Nearly eighty-five percent of the population is unable to read and write any language, and a number of the local languages, such as Sherpa, have no written counterparts.) Something like ninety percent of Nepalis are now Hindu or at least practice a religion which is a mixture of Buddhism, animism and Hinduism, a mixture that is nearly pure Hinduism in the south near India and nearly pure Buddhism in the north near Tibet. However, almost all the great religious shrines in the Kathmandu Valley—there are more than 2,700 temples in the valley —contain icons that belong to both faiths. At Swayambhunath, for example, which is nominally a Buddhist shrine and indeed has an important monastery, also at the top of the hill, there is a shrine dedicated to Sitala, the Hindu goddess of smallpox, at which both Hindus and Buddhists pray for protection. In all the complex and often bloody history of Nepal, there has never been a war fought along religious lines, and religious tolerance is both the law of the land and the practice of its people.

Buddhism was the religion of Nepal until about the fourth century A.D., when the valley fell under the influence of the Gupta kings of India, who were Hindus, and since that time the kings of Nepal have all been Hindu. Buddhism migrated north, through Nepal, into Tibet and China as increasing contacts developed among these countries in the seventh century. The first Chinese mission visited the Kathmandu Valley in A.D. 643. The leader of the second Chinese mission, in 647, Wang Huen Tse, recorded his mixed feelings about "Ni-Po-Lo"—Nepal—and its inhabitants:

The kingdom of Ni-Po-Lo is about four thousand Li in circumference and the capital about twenty. It is situated in the middle of snowy mountains and, indeed, presents an uninterrupted series of hills and valleys. Its soil is suited to the cultivation of grain and abounds in flowers and fruits. One finds there red copper, yaks and birds of the name of ming ming. [Real yaks are never found below about thirteen thousand feet, so Wang Huen Tse was speaking either of yaks that he met while crossing the high passes leading from Tibet to Nepal or of one of the crossbreeds between yaks and buffaloes such as the zopkio and zhum, the male and female offspring of such a union, which to the casual observer look like yaks, but which can and do live at lower altitudes.] Coins of red copper are used for exchange. The climate is very cold. The national character is stamped with falseness and perfidy; the inhabitants are all of a hard and savage nature: to them neither good faith nor justice nor literature appeal, but they are gifted with considerable skill in the arts. Their bodies are ugly and their faces are mean. Among them are both true believers [i.e., Buddhists] and heretics [i.e., Hindus]. Buddhist convents and the temples of the Hindu gods touch each other. It is reckoned that there are about two thousand religious who study both the Greater and Lesser Vehicle. The number of Brahmans and of the nonconformists has never been ascertained exactly.

Curiously, Buddhism was, at the time of Wang Huen Tse's visit to Ni-Po-Lo, a relatively new export from Nepal to Tibet and China. Indeed, the ruler of Nepal, Amshuvarma, had only recently given his daughter Bhrikuti in marriage to the Tibetan King Srang Tsan Gam Po. The king also took a Chinese princess in marriage. (The two brides have become canonized in the Buddhist tradition and are now worshiped in Nepal as the green and white Taras, the goddesses of compassion. Some of the most beautiful

Nepalese statuary shows a Tara traditionally with her hand held out in a gesture of offering.) Bhrikuti transmitted the Buddhist tradition to Tibet and hence to China. In addition, at this time the greatest architectural innovation that has ever been produced by the Nepalese, the pagoda, also moved north. According to Nepalese scholars, the pagoda can be traced back four thousand years in Nepal. It is said to have its origins in the practice of animal sacrifice. (There is still a great deal of ritual animal sacrifice in Nepal. On Saturdays one can drive past the Chobar Gorge to Dashinkali, a temple dedicated to Kali, the Hindu goddess of destruction, located about ten miles south of the city. Here hundreds of Nepalese come on foot and by truck with ducks, chickens and goats that are to be sacrificed on the altar of Kali. The animals, which are led to the altar in a strangely silent procession, are killed with a single stroke of a kukri, the traditional Nepalese scimitar. Almost every Nepalese boy—not the Buddhists, who abhor the killing of animals—acquires a kukri as a sign of his manhood. The knives, kept razor-sharp, are worn in the belt and are used for everything from felling small trees to killing buffaloes. The Ghurka soldiers often use kukris in hand-to-hand combat with devastating effect. After an animal sacrifice, the blood of the animal is used as a religious ornament and the animal is eaten. (Once, in the hills, I came across a small village all of whose inhabitants were gathered around a buffalo which had been hit in the neck with an ax, another weapon of sacrifice, and was slowly dying while the fresh blood was being collected in a copper vessel.) In these ancient rites the animals were often burned after being killed. It was necessary to design an altar that was sheltered to keep the rain from extinguishing the fire. It was also necessary, however, to cut a hole in the roof in order to let out the smoke. Hence to keep the rain from entering the hole a second roof was put on top of the first one—thus, the pagoda. The Kathmandu Valley is dotted with pagodas, often with three or four gilded roofs, resting lightly one on top of the other. At sunrise and sunset they glitter like jewels.

The city of Kathmandu is thought to have been founded in the eighth century. Its name, until the beginning of the sixteenth century, was Kantipur. At that time, according to a legend, during a religious procession a sacred tree of Paradise took on human form and wandered among the spectators. The tree was recognized and held prisoner until it promised to give itself up and to allow its wood to be used in the construction of a single pagoda. Thus, in the center of the town there is a pagoda that is said to have been built from the wood of the sacred tree. In Nepali *kath* means wood and *mandu* means house.

But it is not until the thirteenth century that the real history of modern Nepal begins, with the advent of the Malla kings. The Mallas, assumed to be of Indian origin, acquired control over a part of what is now western Nepal and over the numerous feudal principalities in the Kathmandu Valley. (In addition to Kathmandu itself, and the small community of Bodnath, where the Chini Lama lives, there are two more major communities in the valley: Patan, which has structures that date back to at least the third century B.C.; about three miles southeast of Kathmandu and the oldest city in the valley, with a population now of about fifty thousand, and Bhadgaon, which is about eight miles east of Kathmandu and has a population of about 35,000.) At one point, before the advent of the Mallas, each ward of Patan had its own king, while twelve kings ruled over Kathmandu and Bhadgaon. It appears that the Mallas were of Buddhist origin but adopted the Hinduism of the Newars, the race that succeeded the Kirantis in the valley. (Again, it is not well known what the exact origins of the Newars are and, indeed, when they came to the valley. Many of them have Mongolian features, indicating that they may have come down from the north. But they now practice Hinduism and their social lives are governed by a caste system similar to but somewhat less rigid than the Indian system. *Nava* means "valley" in Newari, and it is sometimes thought that "Nepal" is derived from "Nava." The Newars have some especially interesting matrimonial customs. Sometime between the ages of seven and nine a Newar girl is symbolically married to a tree, so that in the event that she is later divorced or widowed she still retains her status as a married woman. At the time of her marriage, her husband presents her a gift of areca nuts, and if, later, she decides to divorce him she merely has to leave an areca nut on his bed and the marriage is terminated.) The Malla kings were great patrons of the arts, and under their reign most of the pagoda temples and gilded statues that are now the glory of the valley were constructed by Newar craftsmen. The Newars excelled in both metal and woodwork. A typical Newar house, and many that are now occupied in the valley date back to the time of the Mallas, is made of red brick. But the windows and roofs are decorated with marvelously intricate wood carvings. It is one of the sadder aspects of modern Nepal that the Newar arts are disappearing. The brass workers have become plumbers, the woodworkers carpenters, and the wonderful old brick Newar houses are being plastered over with cement whenever their occupants can afford it.

The Malla dynasty reached its political apex under the rule of Yaksha Malla, which began in 1417 and lasted for forty-two years. He extended his domain into the west of Nepal and into present-day Tibet. At Yaksha Malla's death his kingdom broke up again into lesser principalities, and it was not until the eighteenth century that Nepal was reunited. The three sons of Yaksha Malla each ruled over a part of his empire, with a resultant chaos of internecine warfare among their descendants that lasted three centuries. The greatest achievements of this period were in the proliferation of Newar masterpieces as each Malla king vied with the others in building palaces and pagoda temples. In the beginning of the eighteenth century Bhupatindra Malla had built, in Bhadgaon, the Nyatpola, a giant wooden pagoda temple with five roofs, which despite the earthquakes that strike Nepal about once in thirty-five years—the last severe earthquake was in 1934, and it caused the destruction of entire villages as well as a great many of the buildings in Kathmandu—remains intact as one of the architectural marvels of the country. The entrance is guarded by a pair of legendary heroes ten times as strong as an ordinary man. Above them is a pair of elephants ten times stronger than they and above the elephants are two lions ten times stronger than the elephants and above the lions are two dragons ten times stronger than the lions. Finally, above the lions are two goddesses said to be ten times more powerful than the lions and so ten thousand times more powerful than an ordinary man.

While the Mallas were fighting among each other and building statues of elephants and lions, another family dynasty was building its power in western Nepal. This was the Shah family, whose dynastic capital was Gorkha, now a fairly modest town some forty miles west of Kathmandu. The hill tribes who became the subjects of the Shah kings of Gorkha were, and are, superb fighters, and it is from among them that the so-called Gurkha soldiers are recruited. It was not until the middle of the nineteenth century that the British Army in India began employing the Gurkhas as military mercenaries. (There are now about 10,000 Gurkhas in the British Army and, while the exact figure has not been made public, it is estimated that there are about 45,000 Gurkhas in the Indian Army.) Until that time they formed the army of the kings of Gorkha and were used by them in the conquest of the Mallas. In 1736 the ninth king of the house of Gorkha,

Marbhupal Shah, made the first invasion of the Kathmandu Valley. He was badly beaten by the Malla king and died in 1742. But his son Prithwi Narayan Shah, who became king at the age of twelve, took up where his father had failed, and by the time of his death, in 1775, he had succeeded in subjugating all of Nepal and establishing its borders pretty much as they are at the present time.

Prithwi Narayan was a ruthless soldier. He began his conquest of the valley by laying siege, three times, to the town of Kirtipur, a small medieval village on top of a hill a few miles south of Kathmandu. Its inhabitants were firmly entrenched in their fortifications, but Prithwi Narayan offered a general amnesty if they surrendered. They did, and he promptly gave orders that the lips and noses of all males twelve and over be cut off and that the name of the town be changed to Naskatipur—the City of Cut Noses. Only the players of wind instruments were spared mutilation. The rest of the towns surrendered to the Gurkhas one after the other, and by 1768 Prithwi Narayan had conquered the entire valley and had established the national capital of Nepal at Kathmandu. The present King, Mahendra, is the ninth Shah king to rule Nepal.

It was with Prithwi Narayan that the systematic exclusion of Europeans began in Nepal, a policy that was followed, with rare exceptions, until 1950. Before the rise of the Shahs Nepal had been visited, more or less freely, by Europeans and especially by Christian missionaries. In 1661 a German Jesuit, Father Greuber, made a celebrated exodus from Peking, from which he had been expelled, south through Tibet and into Nepal. His journal is a fascinating record of how the country appeared in the mid-seventeenth century. Like all travelers from Nepal to Tibet he had to cross the high mountain passes that traverse the Himalayan range, which forms the common boundary of the two countries. Some of these passes are more than nineteen thousand feet, and the unacclimated traveler experiences serious effects from the lack of oxygen. As Father Greuber wrote upon crossing such a pass, "This hill is of unsurpassed altitude, so high that travelers can scarcely breathe when they reach the top, so attenuated is the air. In summer no one can cross it without gravely risking his life because of the poisonous exhalations of certain herbs." After a month's journey he reached the Nepalese town of Nesti, where he found that the inhabitants "live in the darkness of idolatry. There was no sign of the Christian faith. However, all things which are necessary for human life were abundant and one could there, as a matter of course, buy thirty or forty chickens for a crown." Six days later Father Greuber reached "Cadmendu," whose inhabitants, especially the women, offended his sensibilities even more than the residents of Nesti. "The women of this country are so ugly," he wrote, "that they resemble rather devils than human beings. It is actually true that from a religious scruple they never wash themselves with water but with an oil of a very unpleasant smell. Let us add that they themselves are no pleasanter and with the addition of this oil one would not say that they were human beings but ghouls." Prithwi Narayan summarized his attitude toward missionaries in the formula "First the Bible; then the trading stations; then the cannon." Even now all religious missionary activity in Nepal is forbidden by law, although there are missionary hospitals and schools that are allowed to function so long as they do not make any attempt at conversion.

After the death of Prithwi Narayan, Nepal entered a period of internal political disorder and external expansion. The sons of Prithwi Narayan plotted against each other until finally, in 1786, Bahadur Shah, the youngest son, removed the legitimate heir and became the *de facto* ruler until 1795. It was under Bahadur Shah that Nepal had its first confrontation with Chinese power. The Nepalis invaded Tibet in 1788 and 1791. Tibet was at that time a domain of the Manchu emperors of China. In 1791 a Chinese army of seventy thousand expelled the Nepalese from Tibet and marched over the high Himalayan passes to within a short distance of Kathmandu. Undoubtedly the Chinese then, and the British in the next century, could have annexed Nepal. But for one reason or another, perhaps the stubborn fighting qualities of the inhabitants, both powers chose to administer military lessons and then withdraw. In this case, in 1792, the Nepalese agreed to leave Tibet and to send a tribute mission to Peking every five years, a practice that continued until 1908.

Bahadur Shah was the first *mukhtiyar*, or prime minister, to assume executive powers in the name of the king. From his reign, and indeed until that of the present King, who reestablished the absolute authority of the monarch, the prime minister became, in Nepalese politics, an important and often the dominant figure. Such were the rivalries between the king and his executive officer that none of the *mukhtiyars*, from Bahadur Shah who began his office in 1769, until the rise of the first of the Ranas, the family that ruled Nepal with an iron hand as *hereditary* prime ministers from 1846 until 1951, died a natural death. All were assassinated or committed suicide. A British commentator, Laurence Oliphant, who made a rare visit to Nepal in the 1850s, observed that "the power of the prime minister is absolute till he is shot, when it becomes unnecessary to question the expediency of his measures," and he added that a man's chance of filling the office did not depend on his ability to form a ministry "so much as upon his accuracy in taking aim and his skill in seizing any opportunity offered by his rival of showing his dexterity in a manner more personal than pleasant."

The Shah kings adopted the practice, maintained up to the present King's father, of marrying two queens at once. Apart from anything else, this introduced another source of confusion and intrigue into the government, with the queens and their assorted offspring vying for political power. In their fascinating book *Democratic Innovations in Nepal* Leo Rose and Bhuwan Joshi describe the court scene as it was in the early 1840s, when the power struggle produced a state of almost total chaos: "The royal household was at this time badly split between the King, the Junior Queen, and the Crown Prince. The King was anxious to fix the succession on the Crown Prince, but without his own abdication; the Junior Queen was conspiring to put her son on the throne in place of the son of the late Senior Queen; the Crown Prince was conspiring against both his father and his stepmother in his eagerness to be seated on the throne at the earliest opportunity." To make matters worse, during this period the Nepalese attempted to penetrate south into India, an effort which meant an inevitable confrontation with the British.

The first British entry into Nepal came at the time of Prithwi Narayan. In 1767 the Malla King of Patan asked the Honourable East India Company to send troops to help lift the siege that Prithwi Narayan had laid upon the city. A force under the command of one Captain Kinloch was sent north. Before they even made contact with the Gurkhas, however, they were stopped in the Terai by an impassable natural barrier that the jungle and swamp country interposed—malaria. In Captain Kinloch's day the malaria-carrying mosquito was more than a match for any European army. As a British historian of Nepal put it, "Throughout the hours of daylight the Terai is safe enough. It is the evening that man may not spend in this most beautiful park. Sundown in the Terai has brought to an end more attempted raids into Nepal and has buried more political hopes than will ever be known."

In 1800 the Shah King, Girvana Jadha Bikram Shah, was deposed by his Prime Minister and fled to British India to organize, with the aid of the British, an attempt to regain the throne. But the new government, in order to avoid a direct confrontation with the British, signed a treaty in 1801 with the East India Company, which gave the company special trade rights and, most significantly, permitted the British to establish a residency in Kathmandu. This residency, which in 1947 became the British Embassy, has functioned, with a few interruptions, since 1801. It was the only real contact that the Nepalese government had with Europe and the West until 1951. The first Resident, however, lasted only a year—the Nepalese government made it impossible for him to function—and shortly after he was withdrawn the Nepalese began raiding northern India from the Terai. The border situation deteriorated to such an extent that in November of 1814 Great Britain declared war on Nepal. After several setbacks, a British army under General Ochterlony defeated the Gurkhas in 1815 in the Garhwal hills. The Nepalese delayed in ratifying the treaty of armistice, and in 1816 General Ochterlony was ordered to take the capital, Kathmandu. There is little doubt that he could have done so, but in March of 1816 the Nepalese signed the Treaty of Segauli, which conceded portions of the Terai to the East India Company and which established the British Resident in Kathmandu once and for all. One of the most extraordinary provisions of the treaty, Article 7, gave the British a veto right over any future employment of Westerners in Nepal: "The Rajah of Nepal hereby engages never to take or retain in his service any British subject, nor the subject of any European or American State, without the consent of the British Government."

General Ochterlony, through his bitter struggles with the Gurkhas, had come to appreciate their exceptional qualities as soldiers, and he conceived the idea of recruiting them into the British Army—if for no other reason, to keep them from making trouble in India. This was not done at once, on the grounds that the Gurkhas might have divided loyalties. But in 1832 Sir Brian Hodgson, the second British Resident, again urged their recruitment, and in a communication to his government he wrote:

These Highland soldiers, who dispatch their meal in half an hour, and satisfy the ceremonial law by merely washing their hands and face and taking off their turbans before cooking, laugh at the pharisaical rigour of our

*sepoys, who must bathe from head to foot and make puja ere they begin
to address their dinner; must eat nearly naked in the coldest weather, and
cannot be marching trim again in less than three hours—the best part of the
day. In war, the former carry several days' provisions on their backs; the
latter would deem such an act intolerably degrading. The former see in
foreign service nothing but the prospect of gain and glory; the latter can
discover in it nothing but pollution and peril from unclean men and terrible
wizards and goblins and evil spirits. . . .*

*I calculate that there are at this time in Nepal no less than 30,000
dhakeries, or soldiers off the roll by rotation, belonging to the Khas, Mug-
gars and Gurung tribes. I am not sure that there exists any insuperable obstacle to our obtaining, in one form or another, the services of a large body
of these men; and such are their energy of character, love of enterprise, and
freedom from the shackles of caste, that I am well assured their services, if
obtained, would soon come to be most highly prized.*

In 1857, when the Sepoy Mutiny broke out in India, the Nepalese offered to send Gurkha troops to the aid of the British, and the offer was
accepted. Four thousand men were sent. From that time on the recruitment
of Gurkha soldiers, which the British had been practicing clandestinely in
Nepal for some time, became officially accepted by both governments. By
1908 the first Gurkha Brigade in the British Army was formed. It numbered about twelve thousand men organized into ten regiments. In the First
World War the Nepalese government placed the whole of its military resources at the service of the British, and more than 200,000 Gurkhas fought
in the war and suffered twenty thousand casualties. (Just before the war
the Nepalese Prime Minister complained to the British Resident, "We have
forty thousand soldiers ready in Nepal and there is nothing to fight.")
After the war, Colonel Kennion, the British Resident, made a speech of
appreciation to the Prime Minister in which he said, "I cannot attempt to
enumerate all that His Highness did during the four years of war and after.
Let it suffice to say that in this great war, if the expression may be allowed,
Nepal pulled her weight, and more than pulled her weight." The British
historian and journalist Percival Landon, in his book *Nepal*, written in
1928, commented in a footnote to Colonel Kennion's speech: "It would be
interesting to know what meaning this expression, so full of significance to
any Englishman, actually conveyed to the minds of the Resident's hearers;

for there is scarcely a country in the world in which there are so few pieces of water and boat racing is entirely unknown." In the Second World War, the Gurkhas served with the British on every front, and most recently they were responsible for eliminating Communist guerrillas in Malaya and keeping order in Hong Kong. At the present time the British recruit about three hundred Gurkhas a year, a number that is steadily declining as the British cut back their military establishment. Pensions and salaries paid to the Gurkhas, plus the funds spent to maintain the recruiting depots, come to about a million pounds a year and are the largest source of foreign exchange in Nepal exclusive of the Indian rupees that the Nepalese earn by exporting surplus rice to India. (Tourism is now growing so rapidly in Nepal that it may soon take over from mercenary soldiering as the country's prime source of foreign exchange.)

By 1843 the political situation in Nepal had decayed into a state of nearly total chaos. There were three principal contending centers of power. There was the King, Rajendra Bir Bikram Shah, who has been described at best as weak and vacillating. There was the Crown Prince, Surendra Bikram Shah, the late Senior Queen's son, who was anxious to replace his father on the throne as soon as possible. And there was the Junior Queen, Lakshmi Devi, who, in a secret collaboration with General Mahatabar Singh Thapa, commander in chief of the army and prime minister, was attempting to put *her* son on the throne. The King sided alternately with the Queen and the Crown Prince. In 1843 he made a formal declaration investing the Junior Queen with what amounted to the power to govern the country, and in December of 1844 the Crown Prince left Kathmandu for the Terai, vowing not to return until his father had turned over the throne to him. The King followed his son to the Terai and persuaded him to come back to Kathmandu by transferring some of his royal prerogatives to the Crown Prince. In addition, but still in the background, there was a young army officer, Jang Bahadur Kunwar, who later added the title *Rana* to his name, claiming descent from the Rajput ranas of Rajasthan, in India, a famous Indian royal house. During the next three years Jang Bahadur unleashed or profited from a series of events that catapulted him into absolute power in Nepal and have shaped the destiny of the country to the present day.

The first act of the drama occurred in May of 1845. Both the King and the Junior Queen had become apprehensive about the growing power of the Prime Minister, Mahatabar Singh, and they decided, in a rare collaborative effort, that he should be done away with. For this purpose they selected as executioner Jang Bahadur, who was Mahatabar Singh's nephew. It is not entirely clear whether, as Jang later claimed, he was ordered to shoot his uncle or be shot himself, or whether he realized that shooting his uncle would give him a new status with the royal family, and so accepted the job willingly. In any event, one night in May, Mahatabar was summoned to the palace on the pretext that the Queen was ill, and when he arrived in her room he was shot dead by his nephew. For this act Jang was given command of a quarter of the Nepalese Army. This was only the beginning. The Queen had a lover in court, one Gagan Singh, who, through his liaison with her, had become the commander of seven Nepalese regiments and was in charge of supervising all of the arsenals and magazines in the country. The Queen's love affair became known to the King, who decided that Gagan Singh was to be assassinated. At 10 P.M. on the fourteenth of September of 1846 Gagan Singh was shot while kneeling in his room at prayer. It is not clear what role, if any, Jang Bahadur had in this assassination, but he took full advantage of it to precipitate the next act. The Queen, upon hearing of the murder, was beside herself with rage and, on Jang's advice, summoned all the civil and military officials in the capital to the Kot, or courtyard, of the Royal Palace. She proceeded to the Kot herself, armed with a sword, which she intended to use or to have used to behead her lover's murderer. As the courtiers assembled, unarmed and unsuspecting, Jang Bahadur surrounded the Kot with his own troops. At 1 A.M. the Kot was full. What happened next is subject to a great deal of controversy among historians of Nepal, and the different accounts tend to be flavored by a given historian's feelings toward the Ranas in general. In sifting through the different versions, one gets the impression that the Queen, for reasons of her own, had fixed the guilt on a government minister, one of those assembled in the Kot, named Birkishore Pande, who at once proclaimed his innocence. The Queen nevertheless demanded that he be beheaded immediately and without trial. General Abhiman Singh, whom the Queen commanded to carry out the execution, refused, and Jang Bahadur, taking advantage of the general confusion, advised the Queen to arrest General Singh, telling her, probably falsely, that Singh's troops were even then moving on the palace and that there was no time to lose. Singh resisted arrest and was stabbed to death by one of Jang's soldiers. (One account says that he was cut in two by a single stroke of a sword at the hand of one of Jang's brothers.) At this juncture the situation got out of control, and in the next few hours Jang's soldiers slaughtered most of the nobility in Nepal. This event, known as the Kot Massacre, eliminated in one swoop most of Jang's rivals for power. The King himself sought refuge in the British Residency, and the next day the Queen conferred the title of prime minister on Jang Bahadur. Most of those government officials not already under Jang's control fled the country. Jang had seven brothers and within a few days they held essentially all of the important governmental posts in Nepal. Indeed, for the next century Jang Bahadur and his descendants, the Ranas, controlled *everything* in Nepal as a sort of private family preserve.

Jang Bahadur became, in the thirty years that he ruled Nepal, that country's first really international political figure. The Rana regimes—the "Ranacracy," as it is usually referred to now in Nepal—left so many scars and bitter memories that even now, although two decades have passed since the Ranas were overthrown and the monarchy restored, Nepalese historians find it all but impossible to give an objective account of Jang Bahadur's life and career. There is no question, though, that he was a man of extraordinary physical courage and, while illiterate and uneducated, a man of immense native intelligence, political shrewdness, and wit. Very soon after he seized power, the British realized that Jang was potentially an invaluable ally who, if cultivated, could guarantee stability on the northern frontier with India. Thus, in 1850, Jang was invited to make a state visit to Great Britain to meet Queen Victoria. It is quite likely that Jang's party, which included four cooks and twenty-two domestic servants and which arrived in Britain in May of 1850, was the first group of Nepalese to cross the ocean and visit the West. The visit included a tour of the arsenals and munitions factories in Britain and a review of the troops—both of which were intended to, and did, convince Jang that it was hopeless to fight the British—as well as a night at the opera. The last, according to Percival Landon, produced an exchange with Queen Victoria that became the talk of London. As Landon tells it, "A distinguished prima donna had just given an exhibition of her powers and Jang Bahadur applauded. The Queen, turning to him, said, 'But you have not understood what she was singing.' Jang Bahadur at once replied, 'No, Madam, nor do I understand what the Nightingales are saying.' "

After returning home—through France, where he demanded a review of a hundred thousand French troops, and through India, where he visited a number of Hindu shrines in order to obtain ritual purification for having crossed the waters to the lands of the infidel—Jang, inspired by the British example, made at least some attempt to reform the legal code of Nepal. Nepalese law had evolved from Hindu religious practices and local tribal customs. Mutilation was a common punishment for thievery—the thief was given his choice of having what was left of his arm bound or of bleeding to death—and executions were often carried out on the spot by the prosecutor. (Brahmans were, under all circumstances, exempt from capital punishment.) Slavery was legal, and in order to pay a debt an individual could sell either himself or some member of his family into slavery. Civil disputes were frequently settled by a remarkable procedure involving a "water test" that took place in the Rani Pokhari, the Queen's Tank, in Kathmandu. If the disputants were unable otherwise to settle their quarrel, the name of each was inscribed on a slip of paper, which was rolled into a ball. Each ball, with the name hidden, was then attached to a reed, which was immersed in the deep end of the pool. Two members of the *chamkhalak* caste (the leather workers) were selected, one for each party to the dispute. They entered the tank and, at a signal, immersed themselves simultaneously, head down, in the water. The first man to rise was declared the loser, and the paper ball attached to his reed was opened to see who had lost the case. Adultery was punishable by the summary execution of the adulterer at the hand of the offended husband; *sati*, the practice among Hindu widows of offering themselves for burning on their husbands' funeral pyres, was common. Jang abolished the mutilation penalty and the water test; he made it illegal for a man to sell himself or his children into slavery, although it was not until 1924 that slavery as an institution was abolished in Nepal; and he discouraged the practice of *sati*. (Nevertheless, when he died, in 1877, his three senior wives committed themselves to the pyre.) The method of punishing an adulterer was subtly modified—the adulterer was allowed a moment's head start to flee for his life, an advantage that was, in general, of small value, since friends of the husband were allowed to trip the adulterer as he tried to get away. There was a system of lower and higher courts, with Jang exercising the ultimate judicial power, an intriguing feature of which was that a lower-court magistrate whose ruling was overturned was liable to fine, corporal punishment and even decapitation.

On his return trip from England to Nepal, Jang encountered in Ceylon the English hunter and sportsman Laurence Oliphant, whose observations on the vulnerability of the prime ministers to gunshot were cited earlier. Oliphant was invited to accompany Jang on a hunting trip to the Terai and, ultimately, to Kathmandu, and his account of the voyage, *A Journey to Kathmandu,* published in 1852,* is one of the delights of Himalayan literature. Oliphant and his host did some fine tiger-hunting in the Terai. The method used to hunt tiger and other big game in the Terai, both then and now, does not appear to the casual observer to give the beasts much of a chance. For weeks in advance of the shoot the animals are "beaten"—essentially, herded—by a ring of native "beaters" into a small area in the jungle, which is surrounded by men and tame elephants in order to keep the game inside. The animals are then allowed a few weeks before the shoot to calm down and become accustomed to their new home. At the time of the shoot, bait, which for tiger is a live buffalo, is staked out; the buffalo is literally staked to a post or a tree. When the tiger comes to kill

* The book is long out of print, but I had the good fortune to find it and several other out-of-print classics on Nepal in a remarkable private library in Kathmandu belonging to one of Jang's descendants, Field Marshal Kaiser Shamsher Rana. (Keshar is a fairly common Nepalese first name, but the Field Marshal, who was the commander in chief of the Nepalese Army and an admirer of Kaiser Wilhelm, preferred the Western spelling.) The library, reputed to have been the largest private library in Asia, is housed in several rooms in the Field Marshal's mansion. People who knew him said that the old gentleman—he died in 1964 at the age of seventy-two—delighted in working a conversation around to the point where he could say, "On page thus-and-so of the first volume of thus-and-so the author says . . . ," and then quoting verbatim from one of his books, which he would then produce from the depths of his library to clinch the point. In addition to being a book collector, the Field Marshal was an avid hunter, like all of Nepalese nobility as well as the present king, and a visitor to the largest of the rooms in which the books are housed, on the first floor of the mansion, is stunned by the sight of an extremely lifelike stuffed tiger evidently ready to pounce. On one of my visits, arranged by writing a note of request to the Field Marshal's widow, who then lived in the house, I came upon a live spotted deer in the library chewing on the fur of the tiger. The book collection is incredibly eclectic, ranging from *The Wizard of Oz* to an entire cabinet devoted to works on sex. In addition to an enormous ensemble of rare, handwritten ancient Tibetan manuscripts, the Field Marshal had probably every book on Nepal and Tibet ever written in any language. The library has now been turned over to the Nepalese government by his widow, and on my last visit it had been catalogued, and several other visitors seemed to be making use of the books that are now available to the general community.

and eat the buffalo the stake is surrounded by a ring of trained elephants, which keep the tiger trapped until the hunter, on the back of one of the elephants, can shoot him. About the only chance the tiger has is to panic and stampede an elephant. This is not too common, since a tiger is no match for an elephant, who, when attacked, simply lifts the tiger with his trunk and pounds him several times on the ground until he is dead. (On a visit to the Terai I had occasion to take an elephant ride in the jungle. At one point the beast suddenly knelt on its forefeet as if in prayer. Later, when I asked why, I was told that this was the elephant's defensive fighting position and that it had probably scented a tiger, which, happily, had been scared off by the noise of our party.)

After the hunt Oliphant and his host started the long trek over the mountains to Kathmandu. Oliphant describes the trek in terms that strike a chord of sympathy in anyone who has traveled in the Himalayas of Nepal on foot: "It was with no little regret then that we made the almost interminable descent, apparently for the mere purpose of starting fair from the bottom of the valley, before we commenced the arduous climb in store for us over a range still higher than the one we had just traversed." Finally they came upon the Kathmandu Valley and, like so many travelers before and since, he was overwhelmed by its sheer beauty. He writes:

A tradition is current in Nepaul [Oliphant's spelling] that the valley of Kathmandu was at some former period a lake, and it is difficult to say in which character it would have appeared the most beautiful. The knolls, wooded or terraced, with romantic old Newar towns crowning their summits—the five rivers of the valley winding amongst verdant meadows—the banks here and there precipitous where the soft clayey soil had yielded to the action of the torrent in the rains—the glittering city itself—the narrow paved ways leading between high hedges of prickly pear—the pagodas and temples studded in all directions, presented a scene as picturesque and perhaps more interesting than would have been afforded by the still lake embedded in wild mountains and frowned upon by snow-capped peaks.

As Jang's guest in Kathmandu, Oliphant developed a thoroughgoing admiration for the foresight of his host when it came to dealing with potential conspiracies against his life. In particular he writes, "It is by no means an uncommon mode of execution in Nepaul to throw the unfortunate victim down a well: Jang had often thought that it was entirely the fault of the aforesaid victim if he did not come up again alive and unhurt. In order to prove the matter satisfactorily, and also to be prepared for any case of future emergency, he practised the art of jumping down wells and finally perfected himself therein." Indeed, Jang claimed to have been thrown down a well at one point in his career before becoming prime minister, in an attempted assassination organized by the Crown Prince. By a prearranged plan he clung to the side until midnight, when he was rescued by some friends. (In the Field Marshal's copy of Oliphant the word "dexterously," used to describe Jang's acrobatics in the well, is printed upside down and backwards; in a careful script, with red ink, the Field Marshal, who evidently thought well of his ancestor's feat, has crossed out the offending misprint and rewritten it.) On a tour of Jang's residence, Oliphant happened on a portrait of Queen Victoria and also of a gentleman with "keen eyes and high forehead" whom he did not recognize. Jang was helpful. "See," said Jang enthusiastically, "here is the Queen of England and she has not got a more loyal subject than I am." Then turning to the picture of the man with the keen eyes and high forehead, he remarked, "That is my poor uncle Mahatabar Singh, whom I shot; it is very like him." (This portrait, or one like it, is in the Nepal National Museum in Kathmandu. It is difficult to be sure of the origin of *anything* in the museum, because almost none of the objects are labeled with their dates and histories. Most of the labels are in Nepali, which is fair enough, but even these when translated do not say much more than "Shiva" or "Tara" or whatever. The collection is an odd mixture of old weapons including a "Tibetan leather gun," magnificent pieces of Newar and Tibetan art, and a random assortment of portraits of Victorian figures such as Prince Albert. It seems to be a collection in search of a curator.)

Jang Bahadur regarded the law of succession of the prime ministry— as established by the Sanad of 1856—which King Surendra, the former Crown Prince, signed and which reduced the royal family to political impotence, as the master stroke of his political career. In order to understand the circumstances under which the King issued a decree eliminating himself and his family, in perpetuity, from playing any sort of active role in the government of his country, one must recapitulate a bit as to what happened to the Junior Queen, King Rajendra and Crown Prince Surendra after the Kot Massacre. No sooner had the Queen proclaimed Jang Bahadur prime minister than she entered into a conspiracy with one of the few remaining noble families not decimated in the massacre—a conspiracy in which she intended to murder Jang, the King *and* the Crown Prince. But one of the plotters gave away the show, and Jang had thirteen members of the family killed on the night of October 31, less than a month after the affair at the Kot. The Queen was banished to Benares, in India, and the King, Rajendra, apparently reasoning that, despite everything, he was safer with the Queen than with Jang, went with her. The King organized a naïve and futile attempt to regain his throne, and in May of 1847 Jang deposed him and elevated the Crown Prince to the throne, an arrangement that was endorsed by the British, giving it international status. Shortly thereafter the old King was arrested and brought back to Kathmandu, where he lived out the remainder of his life as a prisoner. The Queen died in exile and Jang maintained the new King, Surendra, as a puppet. During this period a member of the staff of the British Residency wrote that "one may live for years in Nepal, without either seeing or hearing of the King." One may, indeed, wonder why Jang did not simply eliminate the monarchy once and for all rather than preserve at least its symbolic status. The answer is that in Nepal the monarch was—and, by a considerable fraction of the population, still is—regarded as a direct descendant of the god Vishnu, so to have done away with the King altogether would have aroused considerable hostility and perhaps open rebellion among the populace. So Jang was content to keep him out of sight, but alive, in Kathmandu.

The law of succession, introduced by Jang, passed the office of prime minister, not from father to son as was the case with the royal house, but from brother to brother. The first to succeed was, therefore, the eldest surviving brother of the Prime Minister, then the next oldest and so on, and when these had been exhausted the job was to pass to the sons of Jang, then the sons of his oldest brother and so on. The system was designed to insure that Nepal would have a mature ruler at all times. Indeed, one of the problems that had plagued the Shah dynasty was that, since many of the kings died young, their offspring were often infants when they inherited the crown, which meant that the country was ruled by the prime minister or the queen or one of the brothers of the king—whoever succeeded in eliminating the others, usually by assassination, from the race for power. As far as it went, Jang's scheme did at least insure that there were no infant prime ministers. But Jang failed to anticipate the problems that arose from the fact that all of the Ranas had enormous numbers of children, legitimate and illegitimate. According to Dr. Daniel Wright, who was the surgeon attached to the British Residency during Jang's lifetime, Jang fathered at least a hundred children, including ten legitimate sons, while his youngest brother, Dhir Shamsher, had seventeen legitimate sons. A later-day British commentator who was shown a picture of a typical Rana general and his family remarked, "He is surrounded by so many children that the picture looks more like a photograph of a school than a family group." The situation reached such proportions that Chandra Shamsher Rana, who ruled as prime minister from 1901 to 1929, made a formal division of Rana offspring into three classes. The "A" class Ranas were children of Ranas and wives of equally high-caste families. These families were allowed by the caste system to dine with the Ranas, and male "A" Ranas automatically became major generals at the age of twenty-one and could advance—at least in principle—to commander in chief. The "B" class Ranas had mothers who were also legitimate wives but whose families were of lower, though good, caste. These families were allowed to take part in Rana social occasions but were not allowed to eat boiled rice with the Ranas of higher caste. The "B" male offspring became, at the age of twenty-one, lieutenant colonels, but could never rise above the rank of full colonel. Finally there were the "C" class Ranas who were born of mistresses, whose families, being of lower caste, were not allowed to eat with the Ranas at all. Various influential Ranas after Chandra Shamsher, however, made special exemptions for certain of their offspring of whom they were especially fond. Until the end of the Second World War the Rana regime was so powerful that there was very little, and certainly no successful, resistance to it, but such resistance as there was came, in most cases, from lower-class Ranas who felt frustrated by their inability to rise within the succession and hence made attempts to overthrow the system.

Jang was immensely pleased with the Sanad, which enunciated the law of succession, and he commented to his sons and brothers, "I have established a constitution unknown in the annals of gods or emperors by setting up a covenant, and you should not think of acting in contravention of the order of succession. Even if your superior and master takes to tying up goats to elephants' posts or vice versa or to paying no heed to merit, do not oppose him, but rather forsake the country and retire to a sacred place." Needless to say, no sooner had Jang died than his ten sons and the seventeen sons of Dhir Shamsher, along with various surviving members of Jang's family, began conspiring against each other for power. In 1885 Bir Shamsher, the oldest son of Dhir Shamsher, who had in the meanwhile died, organized a coup in which Jang's eldest and only surviving brother, the Prime Minister at the time, was shot, along with most of Jang's sons and their families. Bir Shamsher elevated himself to the prime ministry in a ceremony that was presided over by the then king, Prithi Vir Vikram Shah, who was five years old. From that time until the overthrow of the Ranas in 1951, all of the prime ministers came from the Shamsher branch of the family. (In Urdu *sham* means "equal" and *sher* means "lion." The present president of the Royal Nepal Academy, Balakrishna Sama, perhaps the most important dramatist and one of the most outstanding artists in Nepal, is a Rana. He was jailed under the Ranas for having views that were too liberal, and while in jail he changed his name from Shamsher to Sama, or "equal.") Jang was not only concerned about arranging the succession but also he set about to interlock his family with the royal house through marriage. Indeed, three of his daughters were married to the King's oldest son, and *his* oldest son married the King's daughter. It became the practice of the Ranas to arrange marriages for the young kings as early as possible and very often with Rana girls. Thus, for example, the present King's father, King Tribhuvan, was married to two young girls when he was thirteen, and the present King, Mahendra, was only fourteen years younger than his late father. (Tribhuvan had fathered three sons by the time he reached sixteen.) King Mahendra, defying tradition, married only one wife in 1940; when she died he married her sister, the present Queen Ratna—but they were Rana noblewomen.

In 1854 the Nepalese, under Jang, invaded Tibet, and after a certain number of indecisive battles the Chinese mediated an armistice, the Treaty of Thapathali, in which both governments pledged "respect" for the Emperor of China. The treaty went on to say, "Tibet being merely a country of Monasteries of Lamas and a place for recitation of prayers and practice of religious austerities, should any foreign country invade Tibet in the future, Gorkha [i.e., Nepal] will afford such assistance and protection as it can." In fact in 1904 when the British invaded Tibet the Nepalese supplied them with yaks and porters despite the treaty. One of Jang's more ingenious maneuvers in the war of 1854 was to obtain a declaration from the Rajguru, the highest Hindu religious authority then in Nepal, that yaks were a species of deer, so that the Gurkha soldiers could eat them without breaking the

Hindu law against consuming beef. It was Jang who, in 1857, sent the Gurkhas to India to help suppress the Mutiny; in recognition for this he was decorated by the British and, more important, Nepal received back the portions of the Terai which had been given to the British in 1816. Since the agricultural produce of the Terai is now the most important export from Nepal, it is quite possible that the return of these territories was the most significant act of foreign policy during the century of Rana rule.

In 1901 Bir Shamsher, the prime minister who had come to power after the assassination of Jang's older brother, died and was succeeded by Deva Shamsher. If Deva had been allowed to rule, the subsequent history of Nepal might well have been entirely different and the country could have been a half century further along in its development than it is today. Deva Shamsher was a progressive. He opened a network of primary schools in the Kathmandu Valley, favored judicial reforms and even hinted at the beginnings of some sort of popular democracy. He lasted four months in office and, because of his ideas, was deposed by his younger half-brother Chandra at gunpoint and sent into exile. The only tangible result of Deva's ministry that has endured is the custom, initiated by him, of having cannons fired in Kathmandu to indicate high noon.

Chandra Shamsher was the first Rana prime minister to have a formal education. He studied at Calcutta University, where he learned English. (According to a contemporary account, Jang made a few attempts to learn English during his lifetime and had a fondness throughout his life for having the English and Indian newspapers read and explained to him. There were no newspapers in Nepal.) Perhaps because he had been educated, Chandra Shamsher understood the dangers that an educated population would pose to an authoritarian government, and one of his first acts as prime minister was to close his brother's primary schools. Chandra also maintained the Rana tradition of excluding nearly all foreigners from Nepal. The rare exceptions were either guests of the British Resident or journalists and scholars such as Percival Landon and the great French Orientalist Sylvain Lévi, who wrote favorably about the regime. In Percival Landon's book *Nepal* he gives a list of all the Europeans who visited Nepal, officially, from 1881 to 1923; there were exactly 153. Even these visitors were not allowed to leave the Kathmandu Valley, except for hunting in the Terai. Indeed, the second volume of Landon's monumental work begins with a sort of illustrated tour of the countryside, complete with photographs, which he received from the government, along with a text, written in travelogue style, which he appears to have invented partly from his imagination and partly from what he was told to write. At one point he asked Chandra why none of the English visitors to Nepal, including the Resident, were allowed to leave the valley and why so few Englishmen were allowed to come to Nepal at all. He was told, "My friend, the English have at times difficulty in the government of India. These difficulties arise in no small measure from the fact that in these days of easy travel all English sahibs are not sahibs. Now, I am convinced that the prosperity of Nepal is bound up with the maintenance of British predominance in India, and I am determined that the sahib who is no sahib shall never enter Nepal and weaken my people's belief that every Englishman is a gentleman." As late as 1960, after a decade of intense effort by the post-Rana governments to improve the conditions in the villages in the countryside of Nepal, following a century of total neglect under the Ranas, the life expectancy of a rural Nepali was twenty-six years, and two out of three children failed to survive infancy. It is small wonder that Chandra was not inclined to allow European journalists to learn first hand about the life of the Nepalese people.

Despite everything, it must be said that Chandra Shamsher brought the beginnings of Western technology to Nepal, or, at least, to the Kathmandu Valley. In 1904 Kathmandu was electrified, and in 1906 Lord Kitchener, the commander in chief of the British forces in India, who visited the valley, could write, "There I found marble palaces lighted by electricity and full of Nepalese officers who are . . . always in uniform like a continental nation." During Chandra's regime the Ranas began the construction of fantastic mansions modeled after French châteaux. Fixtures like the crystal clock, chandeliers and illuminated fountain that decorated Chandra's own dining room, which is now used for state dinners, were carried across the mountains from India on the backs of coolies. Chandra's palace, the Singha Durbar, constructed in 1905 and modeled after the Palace of Versailles, contains more than fourteen hundred rooms. It now houses the offices of nearly the *entire* Nepalese government.*

* There is one curiosity in the palace that must have reflected an odd quirk in Chandra's character. Between the main dining room and a rather charming smaller room, used now by the King for receiving state guests, there is a connecting antechamber lined with amusement-park mirrors that distort and distend the passing visitor.

The ruling elite were vaccinated against smallpox. A narrow-gauge railroad was constructed from the Indian border through part of the Terai, and a road was built from Birganj on the Indian border to Bhimphedi at the foothills leading to Kathmandu, and then a ropeway was constructed for transporting small amounts of freight over the hills to the capital. In 1918 Chandra built an English College in Kathmandu, but it trained only a few members of elite families. (Dr. T. N. Upraity, the Vice Chancellor of Tribhuvan University, which is the only university in Nepal and which graduated its first Ph.D. in 1968, told me, when I went to visit the university, that in his class at the English College, the class of 1945, there had been eleven students.)

All of the Rana prime ministers, Chandra included, ran Nepal as if it were a private business corporation. Any income from taxes in excess of the meager expenditures that the government made for public works and administrative expenses was kept by the Rana family, who banked it in Europe and India. The only connection that the government had with most people, who lived in isolation, often several weeks' march by foot from Kathmandu, was the tax collector. Within the country there were private principalities, like Mustang, in the west near the Tibetan border, that were allowed to function autonomously so long as the tax was collected. All opposition, or even potential opposition, was ruthlessly suppressed. Radios were forbidden to the Nepalese until 1946. Most foreign newspapers and periodicals were not allowed into the country, and when a group petitioned the government for a public library in Kathmandu in 1930, the petitioners were prosecuted for contemplating an unlawful action and fined. There was an eight-o'clock curfew in Kathmandu and a similar curfew in every substantial town in the country. Any sort of native talent in the arts or literature was discouraged and, indeed, most of the older generation of writers and poets now in Nepal have spent time either in jail or in exile. Land was held in a system of tenure and debt designed to keep the Nepalese farmer in perpetual servitude to a few large landowners—a system so intricate that even now, twenty years after the fall of the Rana regime, the government is just beginning to make successful inroads in the redistribution of land. A few wealthy families in Kathmandu had telephones and automobiles, but the rest of the country lived in towns and villages that had remained, and to some measure still do remain, as they were in the fifteenth century.

From Chandra Shamsher's death in 1929 until the revolution of 1950, two of his brothers, one of his sons and a nephew became prime minister in succession. In the 1930s secret opposition groups, including the People's Party (Praja Parishad), began forming, aided, both morally and financially, by King Tribhuvan, whose reign began in 1911. In 1941 the then Prime Minister, Juddah Shamsher, tried to depose the King and put Crown Prince Mahendra—the present King—on the throne. The Crown Prince, who was then twenty-one, refused, in an act of great courage. After the war, serious agitation against the regime began. In 1946 the Nepali Congress Party, modeled after the Indian Congress Party, was formed in India by exiles from Nepal, and in 1947 the first of a series of strikes organized by the party began. In 1948 the Rana Prime Minister, Padma Shamsher, attempted some reforms, but was quickly forced to resign by his cousin Mohan Shamsher, who preferred the status quo.

In 1947 the British left India, and with their departure the traditional bond between the Rana governments and the British Raj was broken. The new government of India, under Nehru, was extremely eager to promote change in Nepal. After the Communists came to power in China in 1949, and it became clear that Tibet was going to be invaded, the Indians, who clearly understood the implications of having Chinese power on the borders of an unstable Nepal—after the Himalayan foothills of Nepal are crossed, going south, the terrain is completely open and merges into northern India with no natural barriers whatever—put strong pressure on the Ranas to modernize their government. In fact, in early 1950 Nehru stated, "If [freedom] does not come [to Nepal] forces that will ultimately disrupt freedom itself will be created and encouraged. We have accordingly advised the Government of Nepal, in all earnestness, to bring themselves into line with democratic forces that are stirring in the world today. Not to do so is not only wrong but also unwise."

In November of 1950, King Tribhuvan precipitated the events that led to the fall of the Ranas. All of the King's movements were closely guarded and any trip outside the capital could be made only with the permission of the Prime Minister, and then never unescorted. On November 5 the King saw the Prime Minister to arrange for permission to leave Kathmandu on a hunting trip. What happened next is graphically described by Joshi and Rose in their book *Democratic Innovations in Nepal*:

The Rana ruler agreed and provided the necessary military escort, unaware that among the escort were several whom King Tribhuvan had already won

*over to his side. On the morning of November 6 King Tribhuvan and his
entire family, with the exception of his four-year-old grandson Gyanendra,
departed by automobile from the Royal Palace on what was ostensibly a
hunting trip. The Indian Embassy was on the road the royal party was supposed to follow. On reaching the gates of the Embassy, the King and his
sons, who were all driving their own cars, suddenly swung through the
gates and into the grounds, to the surprise and consternation of those Rana
guards who had not been apprised of the King's plan. Thus the royal family took sanctuary and escaped from the Rana ruler's control. It seems probable that Prince Gyanendra was left behind to avoid suspicion about the
hunting trip and to provide protection for him and the royal line in the
event of mishap to the others if the plan should fail.*

The Ranas attempted to entice the King out of the embassy, and when
that failed they crowned his four-year-old grandson as the new King. On
November 10 King Tribhuvan was flown in an Indian Air Force plane to
New Delhi, and shortly thereafter armed rebellions broke out at several
points in the Terai. In December, when the rebellion had not been con-
tained and it became clear that the new King was not going to be recognized by foreign governments, the Indians proposed a settlement in which
King Tribhuvan was to be restored, a constituent assembly was to be
brought into being for the purpose of writing a new constitution for the
country, and a Rana would continue as prime minister but with greatly
reduced powers. In early February King Tribhuvan and the leaders of the
Nepali Congress Party returned in triumph to Kathmandu, where they were
met at the airport by Mohan Shamsher, the last of the old-style Rana prime
ministers. With this meeting the Rana regime was ended and Nepal began
its struggle to reenter the modern world.

For the next four years the King attempted to create a stable government. The coalition with the Rana Prime Minister failed to work and was
dissolved in a few months; a chaotic period followed, during which the
political power shifted back and forth between the King and the Congress
Party. By March of 1955, when King Tribhuvan died in Switzerland, where
he had gone for treatment of a chronic heart condition, there was a general
deterioration of the situation in the country. Inflation had decreased the
value of the Nepalese rupee, and floods and droughts had brought famine
to parts of the country. There were uprisings and disorders and indications
of a growing Communist movement with links to the Chinese in Tibet.

King Tribhuvan had been immensely popular with the Nepalese people, who revered him for the courageous stand that he had taken during the Rana regimes and for his genuinely democratic instincts. But ill-health and, no doubt, personal temperament prevented him from becoming a strong central figure around whom the diverse and usually bitterly opposed political factions in the country could rally.

Churchill once said, "Democracy is the worst form of government except for all of the others." But in a country like Nepal, where most of the inhabitants cannot read or write and it is a constant struggle for a family to find enough to eat, it is not clear what "democracy" is supposed to mean. It is as easy for a demagogic politician, acting on behalf of a political party whose aims and purposes are beyond the comprehension of the average citizen, to exploit popular discontent to further his own ambitions as it is for a dictator to take command by force. The present government, under King Mahendra, is not a democracy as the term is understood in the West. But a Westerner who looks at Nepal out of a background of centuries of democratic tradition and from a position of great material comfort and wealth should think twice before criticizing the Nepalese in terms that may not be relevant to the problems and conditions of their country.

King Mahendra made it clear from the beginning that he was a strong personality to be reckoned with. Despite the disapproval of his father and the possibility that he might be jeopardizing his own chances of succession, he married a Rana noblewoman in 1952, just after the revolution, when the feelings against the Ranas ran extremely high. In 1955, after he had become king, he issued a statement in which he said, "Today marks the completion of four years of democracy in the country, but it is a matter of great shame that we cannot point to even four important achievements that we have made during this period. If we say that democracy is still in its infancy, we have seen such qualities as selfishness, greed and jealousy which are not found in an infant. If we say that it has matured, unfortunately we do not see it flourishing anywhere, and, I presume, this is not hidden from anyone in the country."

The four-year period from the beginning of Mahendra's rule to the installation of the first elected ministerial government on May 27, 1959, was one of political chaos. There were ten different regimes, which oscillated in tone from conservative to liberal, but in which the King played an increasingly important role. General elections and a new constitution had been promised to the Nepalese since the revolution of 1951, and when the constitution was finally presented in 1959 it provided for a bicameral parliament, with an elected prime minister, but it reserved for the king a wide variety of fundamental powers. Despite the political inexperience of the Nepalese, and the fact that the country appeared to have so much political division, the 1959 elections were both extremely orderly and remarkably unanimous. The Nepali Congress Party, which had been so active in fomenting the overthrow of the Ranas, won a stunning and nearly total victory. The new Prime Minister, B. P. Koirala, was a thirty-nine-year-old charismatic revolutionary, an intellectual (he was widely known as a short-story writer) and, in the spirit of the Congress Party, a socialist. Despite some sporadic unrest in some of the western districts of the country and a few border incidents with China,* it seemed to many observers within and without Nepal that the Congress government was making slow but steady progress with the grave problems of the country. Therefore it came as a great surprise when, in December of 1960, King Mahendra suddenly, with essentially no warning, dismissed the Congress government and arrested Prime Minister Koirala. (Koirala was held in detention a few miles from Kathmandu until his release in October of 1968 by the King.) The reasons for the King's action have never been explained fully, but it may well be that in Koirala the King saw a growing political force that could, if not checked, erode the power of the monarchy. It appears as if some of the younger Congress politicians had made it known that they regarded the monarchy as an outmoded institution. The King, unlike his predecessors under the Ranas, is a strong activitist, and it is quite possible that he found it intolerable to play a role almost secondary to his Prime Minister. Koirala is, at least for the present, living in India.

Since 1963 Nepal has been experimenting with a political innovation known as the *panchayat* system. For administrative purposes the country is divided into seventy-five districts, comparable to counties, and fourteen zones, comparable to states. Each village, or village unit, with a population of at least two thousand elects a local *panchayat* (literally a "committee

* At one point during 1960 it appeared as if the Chinese were going to make a serious territorial claim to Mount Everest, but this was settled in April of 1960 when Chou En-lai stated in a press conference in Kathmandu that the Chinese acknowledged the Nepalese sovereignty over all of the approaches to the summit from the south.

of five," although none of the panchayats as presently constituted have as few as five members) of eleven members who are, in principle, responsible for such affairs of the village as schools, roads and local taxes. There are now something over 3,700 village panchayats, and the number will grow to four thousand when the system is fully implemented. There are, in addition, fourteen "town" panchayats, one for each of the towns in Nepal with a population of ten thousand or more. The town panchayats also have eleven members. Each of the local panchayats chooses a representative to elect the eleven members of the district panchayat, which governs the district in which the various towns and villages of the constituency are located. The districts, in turn, elect representatives to the zonal panchayats. At the apex of the system is the National Panchayat, which is located in Kathmandu. It contains seventy-five members, one from each district, as well as fifteen additional members, one from each of the fifteen districts that contain a population of over one hundred thousand. This group of ninety is elected by the zonal panchayat. In addition there are sixteen members appointed directly by the King, as well as nineteen members who represent special groups such as labor, youth and service veterans. The National Panchayat can propose legislation and debate legislation proposed by the King, but, in the last analysis, it is the King who has the ultimate power to decide whether or not any given legislative proposal becomes the law of the land.

In December of 1960 the King made political parties illegal in Nepal, and several party leaders were subsequently arrested. Most have now been released on the condition that they refrain from political activities, at least in the sense of party politics; some are in India, and there is a certain amount of underground party activity in Nepal, some Communist and some Congress, which could be a potential source of difficulty for the King in the future. During the two years after the coup of 1960 there was a good deal of division in the country over both domestic and foreign affairs. But in October of 1962 the Chinese and the Indians had a serious border war which served to emphasize to the Nepalese the precariousness of their own national existence. "Nepal," it has been said, "is like a fragile clay vessel wedged between two giant copper cauldrons." Since the Sino-Indian border incidents there has been a growing national conscience in Nepal and a sense that the only way the country can preserve its national identity, immensely important to the average Nepalese, is to have a strong, internally stable government, and this hope has crystallized around the personality of the King. Whatever one may think about the loss of democracy in Nepal in the abstract, the fact of the matter is that the average Nepalese, who is a poor farmer living in a small village, has more to say about governing his own affairs than he ever did before in the entire history of the country. While there is some discontent about the power of the monarchy among students, intellectuals and former political leaders in the large towns, where three percent of the people live, it is probably fair to say that the feelings of the other ninety-seven percent, at least at the moment, can be roughly summarized by what a young Sherpa living high in the Himalayas said to me in all simplicity: "We love our King."

Since Nepal has had so little chance to modernize, it is not surprising that one finds so much of the country's history preserved, almost intact, everywhere one travels. Kathmandu, for example, is a living epitome of its past. Every era is represented in a tumbling chaos of palaces, pagodas, gilded temples and concrete buildings—an archeological museum come to life. Some of the impression that Kathmandu makes upon the visitor was captured in a series of articles by Kamal P. Malla that were published in *The Rising Nepal*, the leading English-language daily in the country. Entitled "Kathmandu Your Kathmandu," they had something of the bittersweet quality of letters in a lovers' quarrel, and they aroused a good deal of comment in the city. Malla wrote:

. . . *Kathmandu was never built, it just grew up like weeds. That is why the city takes the knowledgeable tourist perpetually by surprise. He can never tell what next he may bump into after drifting along for a five minute distance from a golden pagoda. The old city abounds in the deposits of time, groaning buildings with beautifully carved but rotting verandas, temples and pagodas in disrepair, cracking door-frames with exquisite details, places of worship with obscene terracotta. It is the art in ruins and disarray, the islands of symmetry in the thick of fuming slums and green gutters, the harmony in bronze and stone thick with pious scum that unnerve every outsider in Kathmandu. Amidst such a mighty confusion of holy cows and mangy dogs, elusive men and markets, suffocating traffic and pedestrians, stubborn street vendors and obscure holes, suddenly there is an island of calm and order, repose and harmony, the work of an unknown artist or artists who betrayed their disdain everywhere in stone, wood and metals.*

To the Western eye, accustomed to cities with a kind of rectangular order, Kathmandu presents the aspect of a perpetual bazaar. Shops with open fronts crowd each other, and vendors selling at the top of their lungs everything from shoelaces to mandarins line the sidewalks. The tiny streets are now thick with bicycles and rickshaws. The automobile is a recent Nepalese discovery and to add to the general confusion the typical Nepalese driver has implicit faith in the power of the horn. Pedestrians, cows, chickens and dogs scurry in all directions to escape jeeps, buses, government limousines and taxis, all honking at each other like angry geese. Moreover, the Nepalese are physically a small people (their average height is about five feet three) and the houses of Kathmandu are also small— dimensions that sometimes give the Western visitor the odd sense that the whole city is somehow a figment of his imagination. The Nepalese are fond of singing, and in the middle of the street there are often knots of people gathered around groups of singers who have come together for the pleasure of it. Above everything else and permeating the entire fabric of Nepalese life is a sense of religion. Religion is the central and sustaining force in the life of the average Nepalese. The city exudes temples and religious statues, some magnificent and some in decay. Religious festivals occur almost continually, and the streets are often crowded with parades in which masked deities are carried along on the shoulders of the crowd. In the early evening, when the city is quiet, people often gather in the temples to sing or pray. Sometimes a holy man, his face distant with rapture, plays a harmonium and chants songs that must be as old as the country itself.

In all of the history of Nepal there has never been a scientific tradition, and the affairs of men and nature have always been seen as reflections of the activities of the gods. Nepal is now entering the modern world; science will play its role and perhaps the religious traditions will alter and, in some cases, disappear. In 1884 a French visitor to Kathmandu, Gustave Le Bon, was struck, even then, by a sense of a culture in transition, and what he wrote seems even truer now:

Before the sparkling but cold illuminations of modern science, the giant epochs of Gods and Heroes that unfold in all these mysterious sanctuaries are becoming pale phantoms, and the world out of which they came, a vain mirage. It is, however, from this world, so poetically strange, that our modern world was born. The pitiless hand of time, and the still more pitiless hand of man, destroys every day the last debris of monuments accumulated out of centuries of belief. One must hurry to study these vestiges of ages that humanity has passed forever. This debris of a world forgotten, whose contours dissolve and disappear in the mists of time, speaks to us of ideas and beliefs of the races that have civilized our own, and they speak in a language that soon man will understand no longer.

2
Fortune Has Wings

$\mathcal{A}$ s nearly as one can determine, there are twenty-four aircraft based in Nepal, of which eighteen are owned and operated by the Nepalese. The international flavor of the list of planes, many of which have been given to the Nepalese by various countries, is an illustration of the fact that Nepal is one of the few countries (if not the only country) in the world where *all* the major powers, and many of the minor ones as well, are actively engaged, for whatever reasons, in constructive, helpful development. Among the aircraft are seven DC-3s of American origin. Five are owned by the Royal Nepal Airlines Corporation—a government-controlled outfit—for the commercial transport of freight and passengers; one belongs to the King's own Royal Air Flight, and one belongs to the Nepalese Army. There is a forty-passenger Dutch Fokker Friendship turboprop used by the R.N.A.C. for its international flights (to India-New Delhi and Pakistan-Dacca in East Pakistan). There are two Pilatus Porters; one belongs to the United Nations Mission in Nepal and is used for official business, and the other belongs to the Swiss Association for Technical Assistance. (The Swiss pilot who flies this plane has been in Nepal for several years and estimates that he has over three thousand hours of flying time in that country, which may well be some sort of record.) These are STOL—Short Take Off and Landing—planes, adaptable to extremely short fields. In fact, most of the fields they use are just that—grassy pastures on which buffaloes, yaks and goats graze until the plane comes in. There are two Bell helicopters and one STOL Heliocourier (made in Bedford, Massachusetts) used by United States AID. These are employed on all sorts of AID missions, including flying animals and fruit trees to remote farms, and keeping Peace Corps volunteers supplied with medicines. In addition to the DC-3 the King has had presented to him as gifts one Russian Ilyushin-14 transport (something like a DC-3), one French Alouette helicopter, one Twin Otter and three Chinese Harvesters. Most of these planes see rather little service, mainly because they cost too much to run. To complete the list, the army has three British twin-engine Pioneers, also STOLS, of which two have been more or less cannibalized to provide parts for the third, and one Russian MI-4 helicopter. A recent addition to the local aerial scene is a Cessna owned by an outfit called the Summer Institute of Linguistics, people who have apparently come to Nepal to try to translate the Bible into Nepali. The Cessna is occasionally available for charter to climbers and hikers.

Nepal has no airfield, including Kathmandu's Tribhuvan Air Port, which handles the international flights, that can operate at night, although a contract has been signed with the Australian government to supply night-landing lights at a couple of the larger fields. (Originally Tribhuvan Field was known as Gaucher Field, which, since *gaucher* means "cow pasture" in Nepali, may well have reflected an earlier state of the art. The present runways are concrete and they are long enough to handle Thai International's Caravelle flight from Bangkok to Kathmandu, although the Thai pilots do avail themselves of a drag chute in landing.) At sundown, all the planes, along with the birds, have to come back to the ground to roost. A STOL flying service is the only answer for many regions of Nepal that cannot accommodate even a plane as easy to land as a DC-3, but until such a service is established (to date, there are twelve STOL strips, and the government is building more) the only way to get to these places is on foot. I was told of a newly appointed district governor who, in the absence of air service, was facing the prospect of a three-week walk with his family, including young children, to get to his post in western Nepal.

So far as anyone knows, an Englishman by the name of Mickey Weatherall in 1947 made the first landing of *any* plane in Nepal. At that time the country was still under the rule of the Rana family and hermetically sealed to foreigners, but some hunting parties were allowed in the Terai, and Weatherall flew into Simra, in the south, for hunting. By 1949 DC-3s were landing on the pasture near Kathmandu that is now the modern Tribhuvan Field. In 1951 Indian National Airways—a now defunct company that, despite its name, was owned by a Rana in India—inaugurated a weekly service to Kathmandu from Patna and Calcutta in northern India. In 1953, the first concrete airstrip was built at Tribhuvan by the Indian Army at a cost of $147,000. At the same time the Indians built a remarkable road from Kathmandu to Rauxaul on their northern border—called the Tribhuvan Rajpath, in honor of the late Nepalese King—and completed it in 1956. While the road is not as well engineered as the Chinese highway built in 1967 which links Kathmandu to Tibet, it is, considering the extraordinarily tortuous mountain terrain that it crosses, a more remarkable achievement. The sixty miles or so of the road that pass through the mountains just to the south of Kathmandu are composed of an endless series of hairpin turns over steep ravines. In the monsoon, many parts of the road tend to be washed away by landslides, and when I traveled over it there were small groups of Nepalese every few miles, chopping up large rocks with hammers in order to get small stones with which to fill in some of the weak spots. Despite the imperfections, the road is in constant and very heavy use by cars, buses and trucks and is the main supply line connecting Kathmandu, and the adjoining territory, to India. That the two roads, taken together, link India to Chinese-controlled Tibet is a fact the geopolitical significance of which is lost on no one.

In May of 1958, the Royal Nepal Airlines Corporation was formed, with fifty-one percent of the shares under the permanent control of the government. Until 1963, when R.N.A.C. acquired the Fokker Friendship, which is pressurized, all of the commercial flights were made with the DC-3s, which are not. The DC-3s still provide the brunt of the air service in Nepal, and there is a sort of homespun quality in the way in which they are operated. I had occasion to witness this myself. I had made a nine-day trek into the mountains around Annapurna, along with a small group of friends and the usual retinue of Sherpas, who function as guides on these treks, and porters. The airfield nearest to Annapurna is at Pokhara, a large market town forty miles southeast of the celebrated peak, and is literally a field, a grassy sward, but one that will accommodate the DC-3s. (Pokhara itself is one of the principal tourist spots in Nepal, with a few hotels—including a modern one that was still under construction when I was in the country—and a magnificent view of the mountains.) Getting to Pokhara from Kathmandu is no problem at all, since the R.N.A.C. operates a regular morning flight, leaving more or less on time, that makes the ninety-mile trip in something less than an hour. The return flight, at least as we experienced it, is something else again. After our nine days in the brush, we arrived at the field hot and tired but promptly at one in the afternoon, as instructed. Around two, a siren sounded at the other end of the field and a large number of assorted animals were driven off what they had come to assume was their pasture. At the same time, a great variety of the local citizenry appeared, as if out of nowhere, to watch the plane land. (In many areas of Nepal people have seen airplanes but no cars—or, indeed, any wheeled transportation at all.) When it did land, a huge ground crew proceeded to unload freight, which I noted included several wooden crates of Lux toilet soap. It was not clear to me how the passengers were meant to accommodate themselves in what appeared to be a cargo plane, but this consideration turned out to be not immediately relevant. Our plane was reloaded with freight, and it took off without us. For the next hour and a half it shuttled back and forth between Pokhara and some destination in the south, carrying freight. At about four o'clock the pilot decided that he had handled enough freight for the day and, after landing his plane in Pokhara, went off to tea. Meanwhile there was a scrupulous brushing of the interior of the plane, and we were told that we could board as soon as the pilot came back, which he did in a half hour or so. We were then strapped into bucket seats along the sides of the plane, given a little hard candy, and flown off to Kathmandu, where we landed just before sundown.

The most obvious application of Nepalese air travel, at least international air travel, is, of course, to tourism. Most tourists to Nepal come from the Indian cities via R.N.A.C. or Air India, or from Dacca in East Pakistan with P.I.A., Pakistan International Airlines. (The introduction of the service from Dacca, in March of 1963, was very important to Nepal's development—which is always guided by a preoccupation with political independence—because it made it possible, for the first time since the closing of Tibet, for foreigners to travel out of Nepal without passing through India. Potentially of equal importance was the inauguration of the Thai Caravelle service from Bangkok via Calcutta in December of 1968, to be followed by a DC-9 service by the same airline in February of 1970. These new jet routes mean that Nepal is now directly connected to countries outside the Indian subcontinent by air. Since Bangkok is on most of the "Around the World" tourist itineraries, the new air routes have been at least partly responsible for the all but incredible increase in the tourist trade in the last year or so. As someone in Kathmandu recently remarked, "I just don't know where we are going to put them all.") Until 1950 essentially no foreigners of *any* description, let alone tourists, were allowed in Nepal. With the overthrow of the Ranas and the return of power to the monarchy, there came an almost feverish desire to make up for the isolation of a hundred years and to become part of the international community. (By now, Nepal has diplomatic relations with nearly fifty countries, and in 1955, after a six-year dispute between the Communist and non-Communist blocs as to whether countries should be voted on individually or in groups for admission, Nepal was admitted to the United Nations. It now has a seat on the Security Council.) The first visitors to the country, in the early 1950s, were mainly alpinists. In 1950 the French climbed Annapurna, the highest mountain ever climbed to its peak at that time; the French were the first Europeans ever to visit this Himalayan region, and maps, where any existed at all, were so poor that the climbers spent most of their time actually looking for the mountain. In 1955 Thomas Cook & Son booked the first real tourists into Nepal, a group that flew in from India while on an around-the-world tour on the steamship *Caronia*.

That tourism got started in Nepal is due, as much as to anyone, to an extraordinary and delightful sixty-four-year-old White Russian, now of British nationality, named Boris Nicolaevitch Lissanevitch, known ubiquitously in Kathmandu simply as "Boris." Before the Russan Revolution, the Lissanevitch family were horse breeders for the nobility, an occupation that went rapidly out of fashion when Odessa, the family seat, was taken over by the Reds. At this time, Boris, who was in his early teens, was training to be a naval officer, a career often favored by the aristocracy; indeed, both of his brothers were naval officers. When it appeared that Odessa was going to be permanently occupied, the Lissanevitch family fled, on horseback, to Warsaw. The situation in Odessa, however, remained fluid for a considerable time during the Revolution, and in one of the periods in which the Whites seemed to have regained control the family returned. The White occupation was short-lived, and it became necessary to find some sort of cover for Boris to keep him from being interred as a former Czarist military functionary. As it happened, he and his mother were staying with an aunt who was the ballet mistress of the Odessa Opera House and a noted teacher of ballet. She arranged for Boris to become registered as a member of the *corps de ballet,* and to make matters more convincing he began actually studying ballet, which he found, to his surprise, he both liked and was gifted at. He remained in the Odessa company until 1924, when he fled to France. After some desultory employment, he joined Diaghilev's Ballet Russe. For the next four years Boris toured Europe with the Ballet Russe, but when Diaghilev died, in 1929, the company disbanded and Boris was once again on his own. For the next four years he danced with several companies in Europe, performed in a celebrated production of *The Miracle* in London with Léonide Massine—a reviewer called Boris "the personification of lithe, sinuous evil"—and married his first wife, the dancer Kira Stcherbatcheva. Kira and Boris became a well-known theatrical dance duo, and in 1933 they were invited to tour the Far East. Their tour lasted three years and took them to India, China, Bali, Ceylon and French Indochina. During this time Boris developed a special fondness for Calcutta, whose clubs, racetracks and cafés during the era of the British Raj were among the most elegant in the Far East. But as Boris saw it, there were two serious defects in the city's social life: there was no place to get a drink after 2 A.M. and there was no private club that admitted both Indians and Europeans. In December of 1936, with the aid of some wealthy Calcutta friends, Boris opened the "300" Club in a palace built and abandoned by an eccentric Armenian millionaire. It was limited to exactly three hundred members, Indian and European, and the bar remained open twenty-four hours a day. In addition, he imported a Russian chef, Vladimir Haletzki, from Nice to provide the cuisine. Recently Boris remarked that whenever one finds Boeuf Stroganoff on the menu in a restaurant in India one can be sure that the chef is someone that he or Haletzki trained at the "300." Of course most of the Indians who belonged to the "300" were wealthy aristocrats, maharajas and the like, who could afford it, and through the club members Boris came to know the Indian establishment that functioned under the Raj. In particular, he got to know those members of the Nepalese Rana family who had built homes in India, often because they had been exiled by the Rana rulers for holding antagonistic political views. He became an especially close friend of a Nepalese general, Mahabir Shamsher Jang Bahadur Rana, who had left Nepal with a considerable fortune and taken residence in India. It was through General Mahabir that Boris met King Tribhuvan, then nominally the ruler of Nepal but in fact essentially a prisoner of the Ranas. Their first meeting occurred in 1944. (During the war the "300" had been used in part as a recreation center by military personnel, pilots and others, stationed in India.) By this time it was already clear to many observers, Boris included, that the days of the British in India were numbered and that, with their departure, a number of institutions, including social clubs for the elite, would disappear. More significantly, since it was the British presence in India and its tacit, or explicit, acceptance of the Ranas that had helped stabilize the regime, it became evident that in the absence of the British a revolution might be expected in Nepal. Indeed, while the King's nominal reason for his presence in Calcutta in 1944 was to seek medical help for a chronic heart condition, he was, in fact, using these visits to make contact with exiled Nepalese like General Mahabir and with the Indian Congress Party, which was favorable to a change of regime in Nepal. The "300" Club became the medium through which these meetings were arranged, and Boris became a very close friend of the King. In 1947 India gained its independence and by 1951 the Ranas had been overthrown and the King restored to power.

Boris had become an avid big-game hunter since first coming to Asia, and it had long been his ambition to visit Nepal and to hunt in the jungles of the Terai. Under the Ranas, though, he had not been permitted to do so, and thus when King Tribhuvan invited Boris to come to Kathmandu he readily accepted. In September of 1951 he flew to Kathmandu in the King's plane. Boris vividly recalls his first night in Kathmandu, when he was taken for an automobile ride in the city by the King and two of his sons. No sooner had they started driving than a leopard jumped across the path of the car and, after staring at its occupants for several seconds, fled off into the suburbs. Boris said to himself, "My God, what a country!" and decided then and there to move to Kathmandu. But first he needed an occupation. Since 1946 Boris had given up the direction of the "300" Club and, among other things, had attempted to set up a distillery in northern India. The distillery had failed, but the experience convinced him that he might explore the prospects for brewing alcohol in Nepal, which up to that time had been carried on on an informal family basis, free of government tax. General Mahabir had become the Nepalese minister of industry, and he saw at once in Boris' proposed distillery a chance for the government to collect some new and badly needed revenues. Boris received a license to import alcohol and acquired the exclusive legal franchise for brewing it in the Kathmandu Valley. On the strength of this arrangement he brought his family to live in Kathmandu. (In 1948 Boris and Kira were divorced and Boris married his persent wife, a beautiful Danish girl named Inger Pheiffer, who is a talented artist. They now have three boys who live in Europe.)

At first, it looked as if the brewery would be a great success. But Boris had not realized that there were well over a thousand private distilleries in the valley and that many of these were owned by influential citizens, who were not in the least pleased either by the new competition or by the prospect of taxation. Pressure was brought to bear on the government and the matter came to a head late in 1954, when Boris' license to import alcohol was suddenly revoked. To compound matters, he was arrested for not having fulfilled the part of his contract which stipulated that he would pay the government a certain guaranteed minimum yearly tax. He protested that to earn the money to pay the tax he needed the alcohol that he could no longer import, but the protest was to no avail. He tried to bring suit, but the legal system in Nepal made it impossible for anyone to bring a suit against the government. Thus Boris went off to jail. He was apparently the first European to have been jailed in Nepal, at least in modern times, and hence it was not clear to anyone what should be done with him. By this time he had become a naturalized British citizen, and at the instigation of the British Embassy he was taken out of the normal communal jail cell where he had first been put and incarcerated in the relative luxury of the tax office itself. Here he lived for six days, among the tax clerks, until he was transferred to a private cell, from which he was moved finally to the local hospital after he had become ill. After two and a half months he was released. King Mahendra, who had succeeded his father after the latter's death in March of 1955, agreed to release Boris on the condition that he would write a letter of apology. Boris refused, but a compromise was worked out whereby the King's secretary wrote the letter and Boris simply signed it.

Several months before this episode, Boris had begun to create the first international hotel in Nepal, the Royal, and had persuaded the government to issue tourist visas. For use as a hotel he had leased half of a former Rana palace. The other half is now used by the Nepal Rastra (Central) Bank for its offices. All during the period in which Boris was in jail the new hotel was being put together, largely under the direction of his wife. Everything—knives and forks, plumbing fixtures, stoves and bake ovens—had to be imported or specially made. Boris was determined to serve first-rate European cuisine, a policy that meant that he had either to grow the vegetables or fruits himself (he brought the first strawberries into Nepal) or to import them by air from India or Singapore. Pigs were a case in point. The domestic pig could not legally be imported into Nepal because of the prevalent feeling that it was an unclean animal. But the Nepalese were very fond of wild boar. Thus, Boris imported a number of white Hampshire "wild boars" from England which he bred and raised. These animals appear to thrive in the valley, and he now has a herd of some two hundred that he keeps in a farm he has in the hills above Kathmandu. A certain number of them also wander around the hotel grounds, along with a large collection of dogs, birds, squirrels and some Himalayan brown bears that are kept in a cage and fed by his mother-in-law—a dynamic, outspoken and delightful lady named Esther Scott, known universally as "Mor." (Her husband is a Scotch merchant-marine officer who is mostly at sea.) It is Mrs. Scott's claim that she was and is the *éminence grise* behind the hotel and that if it were not for her, Boris, whose spirit of Russian hospitality and generosity is legendary, would have long ago given everything away. The pigs are a staple in the cuisine of the hotel, and Boris has visions of moving them to the south of Nepal, allowing them to multiply and selling the extra meat to India. He sees a fleet of refrigeration trucks moving south with the pork, coming back north along the India–Nepal highway and stocking what he hopes may become the first supermarket in Nepal.

Two months after being let out of jail, Boris received a royal command from King Mahendra to cater his coronation, which was to take place on the second of May, 1956. There were to be several hundred invited guests, including newspapermen and photographers from all over the world. It was the first time that the coronation of a Nepalese king had been made an international event, and it became a symbol of Nepal's desire to join the world community. Boris had to fly everything in from abroad, including fifty-seven cooks and a hundred and fifty trained servants from India, six thousand live chickens, one thousand guinea fowl, fresh fruit from India, whiskey, soda, glasses and several tons of ice (there was no ice plant in the country). The coronation and the royal banquet, catered by Boris, were a success, and Boris and the hotel became established fixtures in the valley. Until the last couple of years, the Royal was the only hotel with cosmopolitan standards in Nepal, and Boris built up an extensive international clientele. For a time, his guests included several ambassadors and most of the personnel from the foreign-aid missions, who lived in the hotel until their residences in Kathmandu could be built. Nearly every mountaineering expedition that passed through the country stayed at the Royal at what Boris calls his lowered "expedition rate." Besides feeding the expeditions, Boris has bailed out some of them from entanglements with governmental red tape. One of his prize possessions is a collection of rocks chipped out of the summits of several of the highest mountains in Nepal, including Everest, by climbers who had lived at the Royal.

The unconventional atmosphere at the Royal is not for everyone. The rooms are huge and somewhat cold at night during the winter. Some of them have stuffed tigers on the floor, souvenirs of Boris' days as a hunter (like many ex-hunters in Nepal, Boris has given up the sport, at least in part, because the wild animals are in danger of disappearing as more and more of the jungle country in the south goes under cultivation). The plumbing is uncertain, the electricity a bit on the sporadic side, and the whole affair looks as if it needs rehabilitation. For many years Boris has wanted to remake much of the hotel, and if he can do it he will employ the architectural style of the Newars, the extraordinary native craftsmen whose ancient brick and pagoda constructions are the charm and distinction of the valley. In any event Boris' latest project is the construction of a new restaurant—the Yak and Yeti—which, when completed in February of 1970, was expected to be one of the architectural, as well as culinary, showplaces in the Kathmandu Valley. For his restaurant, Boris has rented part of another Rana palace—there is no shortage of them in the valley—and in it he has created a mixed astrological and Newari decor that should stun the eye of even the most blasé. (When I visited the site shortly before opening day, about a ton of Newari carvings lay carefully stacked on the floor of the future kitchen, waiting to be mounted on walls and archways.) Boris plans to serve such "native" delicacies as Chicken Kiev; choices have been carefully limited since he feels too large a menu tends only to confuse people. The Newar arts, like the wild animals in Nepal, are in danger of disappearing, since, in their urge to modernize, the Nepalese have developed something of a fetish for concrete. Concrete is a luxury in the valley. At present, mortar costs about ten dollars a sack. Although Nepal has a certain amount of limestone and a great deal of water power that will eventually be converted into economical electricity, neither is being really exploited at the moment. (With the help of the West Germans the first cement factory in Nepal is to be constructed at the site of a limestone quarry near Kathmandu.) At the moment, most Nepalese who want to make a show of wealth and modernity build a concrete house, and the government has built a number of stark modern concrete buildings such as the new post office. There is a beautiful old grass parade ground and sports arena on the outskirts of Kathmandu which the government has recently ringed with a rather ugly concrete fence, apparently for decoration. In any event, and even in the absence of renovation, for travelers with a certain sense of whimsey the informality of the Hotel Royal and the personal charm of Boris more than compensate for the lack of modern conveniences.

On a Sunday afternoon not long ago, I went with Boris on a rather typical outing. A few days before, a large British Royal Air Force crew had come into town in a Beverly, a huge cargo plane soon to be replaced in the R.A.F., something like the American C-47. They were bringing in supplies from Singapore for some of the Gurkha military centers in the south of Nepal. As luck would have it, an air compressor in their plane failed, so they were grounded in Kathmandu for several days. The boys put up at the Royal, and Boris set about to look after their welfare. There were daily planning sessions that took place either in Boris' apartment in the hotel— which one reaches by climbing a hazardous looking tiny circular metal stairway from the second floor, and which contains an extensive collection of Tibetan art—or in the Yak and Yeti Bar of the Royal. The latter is one of the prime social institutions of the valley. It is wood-paneled and features a splendid woodburning fireplace in the middle of the room. In one of the planning sessions in the bar Boris decided to take the boys on a picnic, and he invited me along. "We will go to Sankhu in my Land Rover," he said, "and I will show you a wall that I bought"—an invitation that I readily accepted. Sankhu is one of the oldest towns in the valley, accessible only by jeep or Land Rover, since the road that leads to it is both unpaved and extremely rough. It is rarely visited by tourists and is almost untouched by modernity.

At ten the following Sunday morning, we all assembled on the lawn in front of the Royal: about fifteen airmen, two Land Rovers, an Italian staying at the hotel whom Boris had also invited—the Italian had decided to hire his own transportation, which, as it turned out, was very fortunate—Mrs. Scott, and one of her dogs. Boris brought out some wicker baskets from the hotel containing a splendid picnic lunch, several dozen cans of chilled beer and a couple of bottles of red wine. (Wine is practically unavailable in Nepal, and when it *is* available it is usually imported Chianti that costs at least ten dollars a bottle. Boris has experimented in making peach wine and he claims that when it is properly aged it is barely distinguishable from the real thing.) Mrs. Scott and I, the dog and several airmen got into Boris' Land Rover, which turned out to be a rather ancient affair that he had driven, a few years ago, overland from England. In fact, on the way to our picnic its transmission gave out, and we succeeded in getting to Sankhu only by being ferried by the other Land Rover. At a later stage, the Italian was sent back to Kathmandu in his car to fetch a jeep to pick us up. Sankhu turned out to be an extraordinarily beautiful Newar village, and if it were not for the sight of a few modern manufactured artifacts such as an occasional transistor radio or a wristwatch, one could have easily imagined oneself in sixteenth-century Nepal. We picnicked near a lovely pagoda temple many centuries old located on top of a hill, and after lunch Boris took us for a walk through Sankhu. He came to an ancient house with magnificently carved windows and wood paneling. Wood carving was one of the great Newar skills. "I bought this wall," he remarked happily. "The owner was going to tear it down and put up something in cement. The carvings would have been burnt, probably, so I bought the whole wall." If there is a new Hotel Royal it will be decorated with the carvings from Sankhu.

Since 1955, when Boris persuaded the government to issue tourist visas, tourism has grown rapidly in Nepal, and it will soon, if the boom continues, replace the recruitment of Gurkha military mercenaries as the number-one source of foreign exchange (exclusive of Indian rupees) for the country. (The government is said to wish to curtail the recruitment of Gurkhas, since politically it means that Nepalese nationals are being used, or can be used, to fight in situations in which the government position is one of absolute neutrality.) According to an official document, there were 1,987 tourists, exclusive of the few who came overland and were not counted, in 1957. By 1964 the number had reached 9,526 and, if the predictions are correct, it should come to something like at least 50,000 in 1970. The vast majority of these visitors are on around-the-world jet tours and make a side trip into Kathmandu for a few days before going on. (An intercontinental jet landed at Tribhuvan Field in March of 1967, bearing the President of West Germany, proving that Tribhuvan can handle such planes even with its present runways, and there are plans to extend them so that it may become possible to fly directly to Kathmandu from overseas.)

With this influx of tourists, some new hotels have been created and more are being built. In Kathmandu there are two new modern hotels, the Annapurna and the Soaltee-Oberoi. Both are owned by the royal family and are under European management. The Annapurna is run by a Swiss and has something of the conservative good order of a hotel in Geneva. The Soaltee, run by a Greek, is hypermodern. It has four restaurants, one with nightly music, a casino that features blackjack and roulette, a swimming pool and its own air-conditioning and water filtration system. Drinking water is still a problem in Kathmandu. It comes in from pure sources in the hills and is, to a certain extent, treated chemically. But foreigners are advised not to drink it, although there is considerable difference of opinion as to what would happen if one did. Some people claim that the worst defect in the water is an occasional excess of mica, which causes diarrhea. Others say that it is possible to pick up amoebic and viral disorders of a much more serious kind. In any case, all of the hotels serve boiled water, and in Boris' establishment this arrives in various whiskey bottles that have seen prior service in the Royal's Yak and Yeti.

I went with Boris to the first-anniversary celebration of the opening of the Soaltee, which was presided over by Prince Himalaya, the King's oldest brother and at that moment the acting ruler of Nepal. (King Mahendra was in Alaska shooting bear; the Crown Prince, Birendra, was at Harvard, where he was studying; and the King's other brother, Basundhara, also was temporarily out of the country.) It was a gala occasion that featured a floor show, consisting of some singers imported from India, an exotic dancer and an orchestra, and a free gift for everyone in the form of a ball-point pen manufactured in China. The guests, dressed in tuxedos and ball gowns, represented Kathmandu society, the diplomatic missions, important government personalities and the like, and the atmosphere was as remote from village life in Nepal as if the reception were being held in Paris or London. The Soaltee is located outside the city, and it so much resembles a Hilton or an Intercontinental that someone staying there could, were it not for a few wall decorations and the Indian and Nepalese help, imagine that he was not in Nepal at all.

Most tourists spend a day or so in Kathmandu, looking at temples and the extraordinary street scene, and then pass on. Hence they are not aware of how really difficult it is to see anything of the country. A tourist visa is valid for at most two weeks and entitles the bearer to visit only the Kathmandu Valley, Pokhara and a wilderness game preserve called Tiger Tops, in the Terai. Any other travel must be arranged specially with the Home Ministry. Even if permission can be obtained—and for many places not too close to the Tibetan border this is quite possible—the only way to get about is, usually, on foot. For example, it is essentially impossible for the average visitor to get to see Mount Everest; the mountain is not visible from the Valley of Kathmandu, and if one climbs some of the nearby foothills the view of Everest is not very impressive. R.N.A.C. recently has been offering a once-a-week hour's flight in the Fokker Friendship around the Everest area. From the plane one can get some rather spectacular, if slightly distant, views of the Himalayan chain including Everest. It is certainly worth taking, if one has no other way to see the mountains. But it is far from ideal since the chain is visible to only half the passengers on each leg of the flight while the other half strains across the aisle to get a glimpse of *something*. To see Everest well requires a two-week trek to Solu-Khumbu (two weeks each way), some 190 miles to the northeast. It has seemed like a pity that perhaps the greatest tourist attraction the country has to offer is not available to tourists. A forty-two-year-old American, John Coapman, is planning to do something about it. He wants to build an inn somewhere near Mount Everest and is looking for a site with an excellent view; his plans include making a STOL airfield there so that visitors can fly in and be spared the walk.

Coapman was born in India, the son of Presbyterian missionaries, and has spent almost all of his life in India, Nepal and Pakistan, although he lived awhile in Tennessee. Once a professional big-game hunter, he no longer hunts. As he said recently, "The animals need all the friends they can get." Toward this end, he persuaded the government to set aside some one thousand square miles of the jungle in the south for a game preserve. Whole villages were moved out into other parts of the Terai. In the middle of the jungle he built a hotel called Tiger Tops, with the financial backing of two Texas oil men. Its jungle setting near a large river is beautiful. To reach it one flies from Kathmandu to the Terai on a DC-3 and then rides from the airfield to the hotel on the back of an elephant, a ride that takes about two hours. Riding in a seat on the back of an elephant, surrounded by elephant grass forty feet tall, is a remarkable experience, although a little wearing on the bones. The visitor to Tiger Tops is rewarded for his pains with solid food and drink served in a lovely thatched dining room. The accommodations, in thatched stilt houses, are simple but comfortable, and the visitor is taken on long Land Rover rides in the preserve with a chance of seeing some of the tigers, rhinoceri, crocodiles, peacocks, pheasants and barking deer that live unmolested in the jungle. At night, several buffaloes are staked to posts alive, and tigers, if they are hungry, attack and kill the buffaloes—a process that can, in principle, be viewed by the guests from safe hideouts in the jungle. (In the interests of journalistic honesty I am obliged to report that I did not see any tigers while I was there. But many people do, and I saw enough crocodiles from a distance of several feet to make up for the tigers.)

Coapman, a large, immensely optimistic, youthful-looking man, often conducts these tours in person and keeps up a running stream of conversation about the flora and fauna and about his plan to build an inn and a STOL airfield near Mount Everest. He plans at first simply to serve a warm breakfast to the Everest sightseers; later on he will add rooms so that interested visitors can stay and trek around in the Himalayan countryside in comfort. He wants to own and operate his own STOL, which would be the first commercial airplane in Nepal not run by the government. If this is a success, and it is hard to see why it should not be, he is thinking of opening up a ski resort or two, either in the Everest area or near Annapurna. Skiing is almost unknown in Nepal, but the Nepalese seem to be able to adjust to almost anything.

Not all tourists who come to Kathmandu, of course, can afford to stay at the Annapurna, the Royal or the Soaltee. In fact, there is a group of tourists who have started coming to Kathmandu in the last few years whose lack of obvious means of support has been something of a headache to the

Nepalese—the hippies. As nearly as one can tell, there is now an international hippie circuit through Asia that has its ports of call in countries such as Afghanistan, Laos and Nepal, where drugs are both legal and readily available in the open market. In Nepal, the hippies smoke processed ganja —hashish—that sells for about 40 cents a pound. (Ganja grows more or less wild throughout the countryside.) Smoking pipes of hashish has long been a traditional aspect of Indian and Nepalese religious practice, and in Kathmandu one finds a number of pagoda temples in which people gather to smoke a common hashish pipe and listen to a guru chant, or to sing together. I am not an expert on the extent to which drugs are used in Nepal, but from having been to a few of these musical temple ceremonies I have the impression that the practice is largely confined to a minority of the older generation. Young Nepalese are tremendous cigarette smokers, and Nepal produces native tobacco and a vast assortment of different brands of cigarettes usually named after mountains or animals—Sagarmatha (Everest), Lion, Annapurna and Nanga Parbat, to name a few. Many of these cigarettes are manufactured in a plant donated to the Nepalese by the Russians, at a cost of some six million dollars, a few years ago. Like many of the industrial-aid projects in Nepal, it is designed to allow the Nepalese to manufacture something for which they would otherwise have to pay foreign currency. Cigarettes are sold individually or by the pack and are often used for tips and partial wages, especially in the countryside. In tiny villages far out in the hills one finds young children smoking constantly, and every little boutique sells a vast assortment of cigarettes. But one does not get the impression that there is much interest in drugs among the Nepalese. Among the young people who come to Nepal on the drug circuit, however (it is hard to say how many there are, although it was estimated that about two hundred gathered in Kathmandu for Christmas of 1966 and stayed until the government deported many of them), there does not seem to be much interest in anything else.

There are a few institutions in Kathmandu that cater to the hippie crowd; some of them allow hashish smoking on the premises, and some do not. Among the former, the most celebrated was the Tibetan Blue Restaurant (the restaurant was painted blue). It was owned and operated by Tibetans and served Tibetan food, as well as tea and hot lemon squash. Most of the clientele were bearded young Europeans or Americans, along with girls of varying dress and nationalities. The men often wore yellow monk's robes, more than likely purchased in some bazaar in Kathmandu. I made two visits to the Tibetan Blue. On the first one I was greeted at the door by a bearded American from Long Beach, California, who was wearing a yellow robe. At first I thought he must be the owner, but he cordially introduced me to two rather bemused-looking Tibetans for whom he seemed to be working as a kind of greeter. He offered me a turn at a pipe being passed around among the clientele. When I turned it down he said, "Man, if your cup is filled, there is nothing I can do for you," and disappeared into the kitchen. On my second visit, a month or so later, things seemed a lot quieter and the greeter had disappeared. (Recently the entire restaurant appears to have disappeared and most of the smokers have moved over to a new establishment called The Cabin, which also serves "hash candy.") I later found out that there had been a mass exodus of flower people to a site somewhere on the "Chinese Road" (so known because it was built by the Chinese), outside Kathmandu, where they were in the process of setting up an "LSD United Nations." It was rumored that for one Nepalese rupee a visitor to the "U.N." could have his passport stamped "Hippieland." Apparently the Nepalese government was not especially amused by the whole affair, and a recent newspaper report indicated that a number of citizens of Hippieland have been asked to leave the country.

At the nonsmoking end of the spectrum is the Camp, a restaurant and hotel that was founded in February of 1967 by an Indian from Bombay named Ravi Chawla. Mr. Chawla, a friendly and articulate man in his thirties, left a job with Burmah-Shell and packed his family off to Nepal to get away from what he calls "the pressures of normal life." The accommodations at the hotel are rustic, clean and very cheap. The Camp serves American-style breakfasts of pancakes and eggs in its restaurant, as well as Tibetan food, and there is usually classical music playing from a hi-fi set. The atmosphere is more like a café in Greenwich Village than anything else, and the clientele looks and talks as if it might have been transported bodily from the Village. When Ravi was managing the Camp (he has recently given it up), his guests seemed to have a great affection for him, and they expressed it in poems and drawings that are inked into *The Camp Register*, a red-Moroccan-bound book, and are often remarkable. I discovered one poetic offering that appeared to me to have a certain elemental charm. In part it went:

This bloody town's a bloody cuss,
No bloody trains, no bloody bus
and only Ravi cares for us
in bloody Kathmandu.

The bloody roads are bloody bad,
The bloody hash is bloody mad
It makes the saddest bloody glad
in bloody Kathmandu.

And then:

To quench a thirst is bloody dear,
ten bloody bob for bloody beer,
And is it good?
No bloody fear,
in bloody Kathmandu.

Ah, well!

For a Westerner coming from a complex technological society where one is, if anything, burdened by too much communication and transport, it is hard to imagine what it is like to live in a country where both communication and transport are difficult to impossible. Under such circumstances a "country" is hardly a national entity at all. Until 1951, when the Ranas were overthrown, Nepal was a geographical area divided by natural boundaries—rivers, valleys, high mountain passes—into units with practically no interconnection. There were (and are) at least thirty different tribal languages and dialects—twenty of them spoken by fewer than a thousand people each—and only a minuscule fraction of the population could read or write any language, still less the national language, Nepali. Nepalese currency was viable mainly in the Kathmandu Valley; in the north people used a simple barter system, and in the rest of the country Indian rupees were the only form of acceptable money. In many places paper money of any kind was not valid currency; the early mountaineering expeditions in the 1950s that first explored these regions had to take with them enormous treasure chests of metal coins. There had never been a national census—

the first one was taken in 1952–54. Only two cities, Kathmandu and Birat-nagar, in the southeast near the Indian border, had electric power. There was no civil aviation. Until 1956 there were only 160 miles of all-weather and 230 miles of fair-weather roads in all Nepal. The wheel for transport, the electric light, tools, telephones, schools, doctors and hospitals, window glass and airplanes were as remote to the average Nepalese villager as if they were located on the surface of the moon. Against this background, and despite the enormous tasks that lie ahead for the country, almost everyone who has studied Nepal in the last two decades comes away profoundly impressed by how much has already been done.

An incident occurred in 1967 that graphically summarized the kind of social progress that has been made in Nepal. Late in October a new tele-communications center in the very remote Bajhang District of northwest Nepal reported to Kathmandu that an outbreak of illness of some kind had taken place in Naura, a Hindu farming and herding village with a popula-tion of about fifteen hundred scattered over the east face of an eight-thousand-foot mountain. (The mere fact that such an event was and could be brought promptly to the attention of the medical authorities in Kath-mandu is a very recent phenomenon and reflects the fact that most districts of the country are now linked to the capital by telecommunications. There is a dial telephone system in Kathmandu, which in the last few years has been modernized and enlarged with the help of United States AID, and the city of Biratnagar has internal telephone service. There is an international telephone and telegraph service to New Delhi and Calcutta from Kath-mandu, and telephones are being installed in various other cities in the country.) The nearest hospital to Naura is in Doti, the district capital, three days' march away.* Of the fifty-one hospitals in Nepal, most are really medical dispensaries or clinics, and the ones in the countryside are not equipped to handle anything requiring complicated equipment or laboratory analysis. In fact, while there are some 220 doctors in all of Nepal, about 120 of them are in the Kathmandu Valley; and there are four dental surgeons in the entire country. (There is at present no medical school

---

* In the countryside the relevant unit of distance is the number of days' march. Of course, this unit is somewhat subjective, but the Nepalese can walk very fast and very far in a day. To give an example, we took fourteen days of stiff walking to travel the 190 miles from Kathmandu to Namche Bazar, near Everest, but the Sherpas can do it in seven.

in Nepal, but one may be established at Tribhuvan University in Kathmandu.) This works out to about one doctor for every fifty thousand Nepalese, but even this figure does not give a real impression of the situation, since many Nepalese, especially the rural population, do not have sufficient education to make use of the health facilities that do exist and prefer to rely on the traditional practice of spirit healing and exorcism. (It was recently, and may indeed still be, the practice among certain rural people in Nepal to stroke a pregnant woman's neck with a railway ticket—symbolizing the speed of transport—to ensure an easier delivery of the child.) In any event, because of the apparent seriousness of the outbreak in Naura, the Ministry of Health in Kathmandu was notified directly.

The only way to reach Naura quickly from Kathmandu is by helicopter. Since running the Russian and French helicopters that the army and the King own would have been an enormous strain on the financial resources that the government has to spend on its health program, the Minister of Health asked the American AID mission for the use of its aircraft and pilots to fly personnel to Naura. During the first week in November, AID shuttled helicopters back and forth between Kathmandu and Naura carrying medical people, both Nepalese and those from the World Health Organization, which has a substantial program in the country. They discovered that quite a number of villagers were sick and that some had died. By the time the epidemic was over, there had been twenty-seven human deaths and about 150 deaths of cattle. Preliminary examinations indicated anthrax, a disease that is passed from animals to humans. (They also discovered that the people of Naura had instituted, on their own initiative, a quarantine system. The village was ringed off by flags, and each house in the village where there were sick people had itself been ringed off with flags; to cross these flags, the villagers proclaimed, would be an affront to the gods. This quarantine certainly saved many lives.) The anthrax bacillus is very resistant, and since the herdsmen were disposing of the cattle by throwing them into the river, there was a great apparent danger of infesting the entire Karnali River system, which drains western Nepal. It would have been necessary for the government to burn Naura and perhaps the neighboring villages to eliminate the risk of reinfection.

Anthrax epidemics are extremely rare anywhere, and one of the important centers for studying anthrax is the National Communicable Disease Center in Atlanta, Georgia. American AID, in cooperation with the

American Embassy, therefore arranged to have a team of specialists flown from Atlanta to Kathmandu and then to Naura a few days after the first report had come back to Kathmandu. By this time a laboratory analysis from the Ministry of Health in Kathmandu had given preliminary indications that the disease was not anthrax and that the people and the cattle were sick with quite different things—a diagnosis that the team from Atlanta helped to confirm. The cattle were dying from rinderpest, a disease that is specific to animals, and the people were sick with bubonic plague, a disease that is treatable with modern antibiotics. (There has been an extensive rinderpest-eradication program in Nepal, which has been carried out largely in the Terai, with help from the Indian government and which, since its inception in 1963, has been responsible for vaccinating about 950,000 animals. No vaccination program can be complete, however, especially in a country with remote farming areas, and after the outbreak in Naura the government accelerated the vaccination program in western Nepal.) Within a short time the plague outbreak in Naura was completely under control, and several of the people of the village who were sick when the medical teams first came to Naura responded to antibiotics and recovered. Twenty years ago an epidemic like the one in Naura might never have been learned about in the rest of Nepal until it was too late and would have gone on unchecked, with almost unimaginable losses.

Statistical data of any kind are hard to come by in Nepal, and medical statistics are no exception. The Ministry of Health, in cooperation with the Tom Dooley Foundation, only recently finished the first comprehensive medical survey of the country. (One notable aspect of the Tom Dooley Foundation is that it is staffed in part by Pan American Airways airline hostesses, who have been given a sort of sabbatical leave to work in Nepal.) Still, by talking to doctors and World Health Organization officials, it is possible to get some over-all picture of the major health problems.

Since the beginning of the recorded history of Nepal, the Terai has been notorious as the breeding ground of an extremely deadly malarial mosquito. Even now the government of Nepal spends over half of its health budget on malaria control in the Terai. The terrain is so vast that there is no hope of eliminating the mosquitoes in their breeding grounds in the swamps and the rice paddies. Instead the government, in cooperation with the World Health Organization and the United States AID program, has concentrated in the villages. Malaria is spread by a man-mosquito-man chain. Thus, an epidemic can be averted if the mosquitoes can be prevented from passing the disease from person to person. This is done by spraying the interior of all the houses in the Terai villages on a regular basis. At first, the campaign, which was begun in 1954, met considerable resistance from the villagers in the Terai, who did not understand the connection between the mosquitoes and the disease. As one AID official said to me, "How would you like someone to come into your house and spray the walls with DDT?" By now, the "DDT man" is a welcome visitor to the community, and much of the Terai, especially in the east, has been reclaimed from the mosquitoes. A specific, and often cited, example of malaria control in Nepal is that of the fifty-mile-long Rapti Valley—where the Tiger Tops Hotel is located —in the south-central part of the country just below the first Himalayan foothills. Before the United States AID and the World Health Organization, which began the malaria-control program in the valley in 1955, started their activities, the valley was essentially uninhabited and uninhabitable jungle. It is estimated that such population that did live in the valley suffered at least a ninety percent incidence of malaria. By March of 1967 a study reported that the malaria rate had been reduced to four tenths of one percent. In addition, with help from U.S. AID five thousand people had been resettled in the valley, which now has irrigation, medical facilities and a school system; some fifteen thousand acres of land had been reclaimed from the jungle for farming; and with the aid of the World Food Program the Nepalese government is starting fish farms in the Rapti Valley rivers. It is difficult to imagine a more striking example of what can be done, in an area of the world in which hunger is endemic, when modern technology is applied constructively.

Nepal has its share of communicable diseases; tuberculosis, smallpox, diphtheria and cholera are among the most prevalent. The country has made the most progress with smallpox, since it is the easiest to deal with. The Nepalese, with the World Health Organization, have started a mass vaccination program that has had the most impact in urban areas like Kathmandu, where medical facilities are most easily available. It is probably too much to ask that a Nepalese farmer and his family walk several days to the nearest clinic to take vaccinations, especially when he may not understand their significance. Even so, in the countryside one often sees people who have vaccination scars along with others whose faces have obviously been

ravaged by smallpox. A fully effective program will have to wait until a
network of medical centers has been established throughout the country,
and until the majority of Nepalese children can go to school to learn about
the reason for vaccinations. At the moment there are places in the elementary schools for only one in eight or one in nine Nepalese children, and, as
might be imagined, the school facilities are best in the urban areas, where
the medical facilities are also the best.

Tuberculosis is much more difficult to deal with, since both the diagnosis and the treatment are quite complex—the former requiring X-ray
facilities, which are very rare in the country, and the latter a year or two of
rest and drugs, which most Nepalese cannot afford. In the Kathmandu Valley it is thought that about one percent of the population suffers from
tuberculosis. The high incidence certainly has to do, in part, with the fact
that an entire Nepalese family and often more than one family will occupy
one large room. Nepalese houses are small and, at least in Kathmandu, have
two or three stories, with the bottom story often given over to some kind
of shop. The houses are fitted tightly in together, and people often seem
to be popping out of every seam. The population density in Kathmandu is
48,000 per square mile—a figure that is unbelievably high until one actually
sees how little area an average family takes up. (In the valley the density
is 2,163 per square mile, and over-all in Nepal it is 172 per square mile. In
the United States, to give some sort of comparative measure, it is 50 per
square mile.) Even in the countryside, where there is plenty of space, families live in tightly packed rooms, with the result that an infectious disease
like tuberculosis is easily transmitted from person to person. The people
in the Kathmandu Valley suffer a good deal from respiratory coughs, which,
oddly enough, are thought to be caused by air pollution. The valley is a
natural basin that traps the pollen from the crops, so people who are al-
lergic to it tend to suffer. In the countryside there are similar sorts of al-
lergic manifestations; one theory that seems to account for them is that
the Nepalese develop an allergy to the grassy material out of which they
make the thatch roofs for their houses.

One of the long-range goals of the health services in Nepal is to provide good drinking water for the villages. The villagers use water from
nearby streams that are often polluted by man and animal. This, along
with the primitive sanitation habits of the people, accounts for a great prev-
alence of amoebic and parisitic disorders among the Nepalese. Although

Nepalese life expectancy is now thought to be in the early thirties, which is a considerable improvement over the estimate of twenty-six in the early 1960s, almost one child in three still dies in its first year, often from acute dysentery. Throughout the countryside one sees posters in Nepali, with drawings for the majority of people who cannot read, that stress the importance of washing before handling food. In health, as elsewhere, the key to progress is in mass education.

Until the Ranas took over the country in 1846, education in Nepal was always associated with religious institutions. In the north these were Buddhist monasteries and in the south Hindu temples. Before 1768, when they were expelled, a few Christian missionaries founded schools. But in the century that the Ranas ruled, education became the exclusive privilege of the elite. The Ranas imported English teachers for their children, and before the Second World War some English high schools were founded in Kathmandu and the larger cities in the south. The Gurkha soldiers who came back from the British Army after the standard fifteen-year period of service founded a few local elementary schools in the hills; even now in remote hill towns one often sees groups of children being taught, in an almost military rote drill, by an old ex-Gurkha soldier. After the war the Ranas were essentially forced by the example of the expanding drive for education in India and China to provide more schools. By 1951 there were 310 primary and middle schools, eleven high schools, two colleges, one normal school and one special technical school.

It was at this time that one of the most remarkable figures in Nepalese education first appeared on the scene—Father Marshall Moran from Chicago. Father Moran, now sixty-three, founded a Jesuit school in Patna, in northern India, in the early 1930s. Several Nepalese, including members of the Rana family, attended his school, which was modeled after a typical English public school. He was therefore well known to the Ranas, and when they came under pressure in Nepal to do something about the educational system they turned to him. This was in 1949. But Father Moran realized that a revolution was inevitable in Nepal, so he stalled off accepting the invitation for a year or so until there *was* a revolution. The new regime, the monarchy of King Tribhuvan, again asked him to come to Kathmandu and, soon after, he founded a private elementary school in Godavari, just outside the capital. There is now a high school there as well, and the elementary school has changed its name to St. Xavier's. The student body of St. Xavier's is made up almost entirely of Buddhists and Hindus. Although the school is run by the Jesuit order, there is no proselytizing (which is forbidden by the constitution of Nepal). There are about 250 boarders at St. Xavier's and an almost equal number of day scholars. While there is a tuition charge, many of the boys are there on scholarships, a fact that ensures a certain diversity of background. (There are no girls.) The classes are in English, and the level is such that a boy who does well at St. Xavier's can go to an English or American university and not be at a competitive disadvantage.

Father Moran is an enormously popular figure in Kathmandu. A few years ago King Mahendra conferred Nepalese citizenship on him, making him, to date, the only American to be so honored. He is an enthusiastic radio ham, and when I went to Godavari to have tea with him at the school, a former Rana palace, I was ushered into his radio room. He told me that he is a link in an international amateur communication system that extends all over Asia. He was waiting for his nightly signal from Singapore that would tell him if there were any messages to pass on to the next ham in the chain. (During the American Everest expedition of 1963, his station, 9NIMM, was one of the few links of the climbers to the outside world.) While we were drinking tea he was twiddling with various dials, and after a few minutes he got his call from Singapore, which said that there was nothing on the line, a bit of information that he passed on to the next member in the relay. Afterward he introduced me to a number of the boys, who spoke excellent English and seemed extremely bright. One of them was a young Sherpa from the hills whom Father Moran persuaded to sing a lovely Nepalese song. When I left, Father Moran, who had once been a premedical student, was on his way to make some sick rounds in the school. After seeing him in action for an hour or so, one gets the impression that he can do about anything he sets his mind to.

Father Moran is in the business of quality education, which, in an underdeveloped country, especially one such as Nepal where there is already an elite traditional class of educated people, is, in a sense, the easiest to provide, since only a relatively small number of people are involved. In principle, elementary education is compulsory in Nepal, but in practice there is an acute shortage of elementary schools and schoolteachers, especially in the countryside. It is probable that no more than twenty or thirty percent of the children now go to school, although the number is steadily growing.

In 1965 a survey indicated that there were 5,364 primary schools, as opposed to 310 in 1951, and 270 high schools as opposed to 22. There are also 42 degree "colleges" in the country, most of them liberal arts colleges granting a B.A. degree. Even in the Kathmandu Valley, where the educational facilities are the best in the country, young children do not necessarily go to school. If one stands in the morning by one of the bridges that lead into Kathmandu over the rivers that bound the city, one sees streams of children driving animals to market or coming into town to work.

Apart from the shortage of facilities, one of the most acute problems in Nepal is that young people who might become teachers and who might contribute to the development of the villages often view education as a means to escape village life for the relative comfort and sophistication of the cities like Kathmandu. This attitude becomes more pronounced as students move up the educational ladder and is very extreme at the university level. There is only one university in the country, Tribhuvan University, which was founded, with the help of U.S. AID funds, in 1959. Several colleges affiliated with the university are located in towns outside Kathmandu, but the principal activities of the university, and especially its graduate schools, are in the valley. There are now some six thousand students at the university and since 1966 they have been attending classes in a new campus constructed a few miles south of the city. Shortly before the new campus opened I paid a visit to Vice Chancellor Upraity, whose office is in one of its attractive new buildings. Dr. Upraity received his undergraduate education in the English College in Kathmandu, took his doctorate at the University of Oregon and then returned to Nepal, where he became involved with education. Now one of his principal concerns is the placement of university graduates. Many of them want to stay in Kathmandu, where, if they have been educated in the social sciences, the only career really open to them is with the national government, and such positions have been largely saturated—a situation that is a source of potential frustration among the students. It is aggravated by the fact that students (like everyone else) have been forbidden by law to engage in party politics. Parties were outlawed by King Mahendra in 1961, and many of their leaders were imprisoned. Most have now been released and the university students tend to gravitate toward the more dynamic of them. The present political system, centered on the local *panchayats*, does not seem to have captured the imagination of the students, and there has been a certain amount of agitation that has led to some student strikes and to the imprisonment of student leaders. King Mahendra has been very skillful in incorporating opposition leaders into his government, and it is said that some students feel that the best route into the government is to attract attention by agitation. The King is now encouraging a Go-to-the-Village campaign aimed at convincing students and others that they can best contribute to the development of Nepal by bringing their talents to bear on village problems. The paradox is that the more highly trained a man becomes, the less relevant are his skills to the condition of the villages. At its present stage of development Nepal does not need highly trained engineers as much as it needs people who can and will construct simple wooden bridges; it does not need highly trained biologists as much as it needs people who can convince farmers to try new seeds; and it does not need doctors who have been trained to cope with Western medical problems, the diseases of technological civilizations where the life expectancy is twice what it is in Nepal, but it needs people who are willing to teach elementary sanitation in the villages in the hills. The present overproduction of intellectuals is not acute, since the number of Nepalese who are being trained at the university level is such a minuscule fraction of the population, but unless the development of the country can keep pace with the increasing educational opportunities, Dr. Upraity's graduates will be forced to go abroad to practice their professions.

One of the most effective outfits working with the Nepalese in an effort to improve their educational system is the American Peace Corps. In 1963 an unnamed American author writing in an official publication made an attempt to assess the Nepalese impression of Americans. He noted: "A fairly large number of Nepalese have had some form of contact with Americans, mainly with tourists or those composing the official mission. The general stereotype which has arisen from this acquaintance depicts them as good-hearted, generous and friendly but basically simple people of somewhat limited perception." He went on to say, "According to all reports, volunteers of the United States Peace Corps have already had a measurable effect in improving the image of the United States."

It is my impression that for the people in the countryside of Nepal, the Peace Corps volunteers now *are* the image of the United States. Wherever one goes in the back country of Nepal, if one says that one is an American it is almost immediately assumed that one must be in the Peace Corps. There are now about 230 volunteers in Nepal, and the Nepalese government has asked for fifty more. The volunteers go only where the Nepalese government asks them to go, and they work in fields chosen by the Nepalese. At present they are working in agriculture, rural construction—bridges and roads—and education. The volunteers arrive in Nepal with a certain minimum skill in Nepali, and in a few months—they are generally there for a minimum of eighteen months—they become fluent and often learn one of the local languages as well. When they go into a village they usually work in collaboration with a Nepalese counterpart engaged in the same activity and share the experiences of primitive village life. I spoke to several volunteers who teach school. In one case there was a husband-and-wife team from the Bronx. He teaches elementary school in the Kathmandu Valley, and she has organized the first school in Nepal for deaf children. Another young volunteer whom I met had had mathematical training and was attempting to write an elementary modern textbook in high-school mathematics, in Nepali, for use in the schools; he had, incidentally, chosen to live in a typical village house with no electricity or running water and with a straw mat to sleep on, although he was working near Kathmandu. In all instances, they stressed the fact that their major obstacle is the emphasis that has been placed in the past on rote. The Nepalese consider a man educated if he can recite by heart large parts of religious texts; no one ever taught children how to solve problems. The volunteers try to emphasize teaching children to deal with new and unfamiliar situations by reasoning them out. There was also a feeling among the volunteers that the Nepalese schools tend to teach English too soon. It is quite customary to start English in the third grade—a procedure that might be all right except that many of the children do not yet speak their national language, Nepali, and so are forced to learn two languages at once.

In agriculture, the volunteers try to persuade the villagers to try new things—new seeds, new techniques for combating plant diseases, and the like. Young Americans are simply not used to a society in which progress is regarded as impossible, and perhaps the greatest contribution that the volunteers can therefore make is in sharing their optimism and opening up new options for the villagers. Simply giving practical demonstrations of how one goes about trying to solve problems is invaluable in a society in which people have been resigned to accepting the conditions of the past as inevitable. In general the Peace Corps volunteers fall in love with Nepal—

with the beauty of the countryside and with the charm and kindness of the people—and a substantial proportion of them stay on for a second tour of duty. Indeed, after leaving the Peace Corps many of them try to come back to Nepal to work with outfits like U.S. AID.

Most of the people I spoke to in our AID mission acknowledge that the first Americans to come to Nepal in 1952 to set up what was then the United States Technical Co-operation Mission seriously underestimated the difficulties of the job. At that time it was generally assumed that the people were aware of the possibilities of development—that they shared a "rising tide of expectations"—and that if they were shown what to do they would set off by themselves and do it. What in fact the U.S. AID missions found was that the people had, in general, no expectations at all and that there was, if anything, a profound resistance to change. This attitude meant that the only way to ensure the continuity of a project was for the advisers simply to commit themselves to running it indefinitely. In fact, many of the larger projects involving machines and mechanized factories, completely unfamiliar to the Nepalese, simply stopped once they were turned over to the local people. For this reason, and because the battle to build and stabilize the Nepalese economy will be won or lost in rural Nepal, U.S. AID is now focusing most of its effort in rural development. The annual AID budget in Nepal now runs to about ten million dollars, more than two thirds of which is given to the Nepalese in American-owned Indian rupees; the largest item in the budget is agriculture.

Nepal is one of the few countries in Asia which produces a surplus of food. This surplus is in the form of cereal grains—wheat, rice, millet—and in a normal year comes to about 330,000 metric tons. It is sold to northern India, where there are chronic food shortages, especially in recent years in which there have been droughts and then floods. Food export is the country's largest source of income. If this were all there were to the agricultural situation, it would look quite bright. The problem is that the surplus is grown in the south, where the land is flat and agriculturally rich, but only about a third of the people live in the south. Two thirds live in the hills in the north, where there is a food shortage that must be met by importing food from the south. In 1965 the deficit in the hills was estimated to be 230,000 metric tons, and what is shipped to India represents the excess cultivated in the Terai—the south—over what is needed to feed the rest of the population. This unbalance might be tolerated except that the birth rate in the hills is increasing faster than the rate of food production: in the hills the population is growing at a rate of about two and a half percent a year, while food production is increasing by about one percent a year. Moreover, as medical services improve and as the Nepalese enrich their diets (Nepalese, typically, now eat two meals a day, which are usually based on rice, millet or potatoes—there is relatively little consumption of meat and vegetables), the population will grow even faster without a compensating increase in agricultural production. As it is, in about 1978 Nepal will turn from a surplus-food country to a deficit-food country if nothing changes.

The situation is compounded by the transportation problem. Essentially everything that goes in and out of the hills is now carried on people's backs. This means that, because of the expense of transportation, prices are raised at either end. But the people in the hills have relatively few methods of earning cash; the most important is mercenary soldiering, which is gradually diminishing. Hence many hill people have already been forced to move south into the Terai—indeed, the Rapti Valley project is largely populated by resettled hill people—and others have emigrated to India. There is a good deal of seasonal migration back and forth across the southern borders for purposes of finding work. The government is confronted with a dilemma, since to reduce the cost of living in the hills it is essential to build roads there, but if the country builds roads it may simply help to perpetuate a situation that is fundamentally unsound economically. As one official puts it, "Is it a good idea to build a road that doesn't go anywhere?" Various plans are now under study, including the introduction of new hill crops such as apples or tea. The climate in the lower Himalayan foothills is so diverse that almost anything will probably grow somewhere.

The most obvious things that the country has to do if it is to continue to have a food surplus are to increase food production and to decrease the birth rate. Family planning is just beginning in Nepal, and U.S. AID is cooperating in this program with the Ministry of Health. In Nepal, as in most underdeveloped countries, the problem is one of education coupled with a feeling among the people that because of the high death rates among children it is necessary to have large families in order to insure the survival of some offspring into adulthood. (There do not seem to be any religious barriers among the Nepalese to family planning and they seem to accept the idea more readily than do Indian families.) While there is a good deal written about family planning in the press, and while it is included as part of the Go-to-the-Village program, one does not get the impression that it is being dealt with as yet on a scale large enough or with sufficient urgency to make much of a dent. On the other hand, the program to grow more food *is* having successes.

To increase food production requires both incentive and technology, and on both counts the Nepalese situation is extremely complex. Nepal has one of the most intricate land-tenure systems in all of Asia. It is probably fair to summarize the matter by saying that in general about the only thing that is clear in connection with the ownership of land is that it is not owned by the tiller. Under the Ranas, land was given to all sorts of people and institutions on the condition that some fraction of the revenues be turned back to them. Hence large blocks of land were held by individual landlords who rented it out, often for rates consuming as much as eighty percent of the production. In addition, a tenant could be removed from the land more or less at the will of the landlord. Under such circumstances, it is hardly any wonder that the average farmer had little or no incentive to try to increase his production. Beginning in 1955, the government started a land-reform program that led to the proclamation of the Lands Act of 1957, which limited the landlord's rent to fifty percent of the produce and gave the tenant a good deal of protection and security. But it did not do anything about the accumulation of huge landholdings by individual landlords and their families. Hence, in 1964 a new Lands Act was passed that limited such holdings. Now, Nepalese units of measurement have been known to make strong men weep—the country is now engaged in a campaign to introduce the metric system to facilitate international trade—and this applies to the units of land area. Limitations on landholdings have been given in terms of the traditional Nepalese units, the *bigha* and the *ropani*. The maximum amount of land that any single owner can hold is twenty-five *bigha*s where a *bigha* is about 1.6 acres; thus, the maximum holding is just over forty acres. But in the Kathmandu Valley, where land is very valuable, the landholder can hold only 50 *ropani*s. The *ropani* is equal to 608⅘ square yards, while a *bigha* comes to 8,100 square yards. Excess land is to be purchased by the government and redistributed. A tenant who has cultivated an annual crop at least once cannot be evicted by the landholder on "arbitrary grounds," and the annual rent cannot exceed fifty percent of the produce and cannot be raised to fifty percent if it has been traditionally less on a given plot. It is generally agreed in Nepal that this is an excellent law, and the King has put behind it the full weight of his authority and his conviction about the need for land reform.

In practice, the law has been difficult to carry out. This is due in part to the fact that the Nepalese and, above all, the rural Nepalese, do not think quantitatively. Almost everyone who has traveled in rural Nepal has noticed how difficult it is to find out the distance to any place, even by asking people who live in the area. The farmers do not have the habit of measuring distances and areas, and the problem of learning who owns what certainly stems in part from the fact that plots of land have been only vaguely defined. Part of the problem also stems from deliberate attempts on the part of the landowners to conceal ownership by dividing their holdings among in-laws and the like. A Nepalese "family" is often a very extensive unit that includes many "families" in the Western sense of the term. Hence one of the most important aspects of the land-reform program is to make surveys of the land to find out, in detail, who really owns it. Despite the difficulties, these surveys have been, or are being, carried out throughout Nepal, and a report in 1967 indicated that 537,120 farmers had been issued provisional land-tenancy certificates, that 90,064 *bighas* of excess land had been taken over by the government, and that 15,408 *bighas* had been redistributed to farmers. In addition, the government has taken steps to provide incentive for the farmers to increase production. In the Kathmandu Valley, for example, the traditional main crop has been rice. It is planted at the beginning of the summer monsoon and harvested in the fall. During the winter the fertile fields had been allowed, more or less, to lie idle. In recent years, with the help of AID, the farmers in the valley have been encouraged to plant wheat as a winter crop. To provide incentive the government has restricted the rent that the tenant pays to a percentage of the main crop only, so that a farmer who grows wheat as well as the main rice crop can keep the proceeds from the wheat for his family. New strains of winter wheat have been introduced into the valley, with the result that as of 1967 the Kathmandu Valley, long a food-deficit area, became, for the first time, a surplus-food area, producing 2,254 metric tons of surplus. To accommodate this, grain-storage facilities—*gowdowns*—have been built in the valley (the Chinese have constructed *gowdowns* and warehouses both in the Kathmandu Valley and in the south as part of *their* aid program for Nepal) to counteract the adverse effects of seasons of drought. In the past, the Nepalese have been forced to import grain from abroad in bad seasons.

Along with the land-reform program, the government has instituted a compulsory savings program for farmers. It is designed to generate credit for farm investment and to free the Nepalese farmer from his traditional heavy indebtedness. For generations Nepalese farmers have been victimized when they have had to borrow money. In many cases the initial loan was to pay for a wedding ceremony or some other important social event, and because of escalating scales of interest the farmer was soon in debt for life. It has been, until recently, very rare for a farmer to borrow money for farm development—the purchase of fertilizers, seeds and the like—since there was no way he could do this without being usurized. So long as he was earning so little for working on the land, the Nepalese farmer was not motivated to develop it. The compulsory savings program, which may be unique among developing countries, began in 1964 when the government simply decreed that, in the case of a rice paddy, the major Nepalese crop, a farmer would be required to set aside a certain fraction of his yield as savings. For rice the fraction, in Nepalese units, is one *maund* per *bigha* where a *maund* is equivalent to about eighty-two pounds. This could be turned over to the savings association either in cash or in rice, which was then stored. In order to get the farmers to comply, the land-reform officer frequently showed up accompanied by an armed soldier and said to the farmer, "Where is your paddy?" The savings are completely distinct from a tax. The money belongs to the farmer, or is eventually available to him, and he earns interest on it. In only three years, well over thirteen million dollars was accumulated this way—a staggeringly large sum when one realizes that the entire assets of the Nepal Rastra Bank are about fifty million dollars. It is even more remarkable that this program was under the direction of a Nepalese, Mohan Man Sainju, who is now in his late twenties and is currently studying for a Ph.D. at the University of North Carolina.

I had a chance to pay a visit to Mr. Sainju in his office in the Singha Durbar, the labyrinthine palace which houses essentially all of the central government. An uninitiated visitor can get hopelessly lost in the place, and I was fortunate to have as a guide Dr. Raymond Fort, who is in charge of the Rural Development Division of the United States AID program in Nepal. Dr. Fort grew up on a farm in the Midwest and is very familiar with the problems of farming and farmers. He is also an old friend of

Sainju. Sainju's office turned out to be a simple room with a cloth curtain for a door, and Sainju himself a delightfully informal man who looked even younger than his age. He had been educated in Nepal, and Fort remarked after our visit that this might have been a very good thing, since he had been able to come up with original solutions to Nepalese problems without preconceptions that he might have had if he had studied Western methods that did not necessarily apply to the local situation. Sainju told us that his department was working on formulating the best methods for returning the money to the farmers in the form of low-interest loans or credits. On the one hand, if this is done without close supervision the money may be used, as in the past, for weddings and other nondevelopmental expenditures; and, on the other hand, if the money is supervised federally it means increasing the burdens of the central government and retarding the development of local self-government. Like most Nepalese whom I met in the government, Sainju believes in strengthening the *panchayat* system, so that eventually each village can take the responsibility for its own development program and can raise its own local taxes to be used for the construction of local roads, schools and medical centers. At the moment most of these things are done at the federal level, with a considerable loss of efficiency. Farmers are now beginning to take advantage of the development funds, which they use to buy new seeds and fertilizer, and Fort told me that in some areas production has increased by a factor of ten in three years. I asked Sainju what the main difficulties were that the program faced. He thought that education was the most serious problem. As he put it, "In some households a farmer wants to try new seeds, but his wife believes that if he plants them then the gods will kill her oldest son."

There is a difference of opinion in Nepal as to how successfully—and when, if ever—the country can be industrialized. Nepal has some mineral resources, including iron, lead and nickel. There is some mica, limestone, gold, oil and natural gas, but in many cases these deposits are located in areas that are so remote that even if they were worked they could not be economically exploited. The dream, shared by many, that somewhere under the Himalayas enormous deposits of precious metals, perhaps even uranium, would be found has so far not materialized. Apart from the soil, the main resources of the country appear to be water power and the forests. About one third of the country is estimated to be forest land. Sal, sisau, semal, khair, karma and asna trees grow in the south. Salwood has long been sold to India, where it is used for, among other things, the construction of railway sleepers. Sisauwood is used for making furniture, and semal, a soft wood, is used for making matches. (In fact, the matches that one buys in Nepal are so soft that they often break in two before one can light them.) In the north the countryside is covered with marvelous forests of evergreens and oaks, but again, because of the difficulty of transportation, they are not being utilized. The forests in the south are in danger of disappearing, since they have been exploited for generations without thought of conservation. This despoiling has contributed to a great deal of land erosion in the southern hills, and the Nepalese are now making a major effort to conserve and reclaim the forests. In 1957 the government established a Forest Nationalization Act, which brought the forests under federal control, and a forest survey is now being completed so that the extent and value of the forests will be known more precisely. On the other hand, Nepal has one of the greatest potential hydroelectric-power sources in the world in the rivers that flow south from the Himalayas. In this respect, like so many others, Nepal resembles Switzerland, also a land-locked country with enormous power resources. Switzerland, of course, is highly industrialized and can sell its surplus power to rich neighbors who are, if anything, even more highly industrialized. Nepal's northern neighbor, Tibet, is less industrialized than Nepal itself, which makes India the only potential customer for surplus electric power. Indeed, India has already helped to build several hydroelectric plants in Nepal, and plans have been made to build an enormous power system in the west making use of the Karnali River. An important side effect of these power projects will be the dams that can be used to store water for irrigation. Nepal has very heavy rainfall during the summer months—the monsoon—but relatively little during the winter, and water storage will be an invaluable aid to the farmers.

Apart from the existence, or nonexistence, of natural resources, there are other uncertainties to the future industrialization of the country. Both India and China mass-produce consumer items such as shoes, cooking utensils, fountain pens, soap and automobiles. (Most of the trucks that one sees in Nepal are Mercedes trucks that are made in the Indian Tata automobile works.) It is very unlikely that the Nepalese can produce these things at competitive prices for export in the near future. Therefore, there is now emphasis on building industries for import substitution—that is, manufacturing things for the Nepalese market that would otherwise have to be imported, and thus saving the valuable foreign currency that Nepal earns. There have already been some successes with this in matches, cigarettes, sugar, textiles and soap, and soon there will be other "substitution" industries such as the new cement plant near Kathmandu. The largest uncertainty in the industrial development of the country is, perhaps, the question of whether an agrarian people can adjust to the requirements of working in factories. Some people say that the Nepalese are so devoted to the land that it is unlikely that they will ever make successful industrial workers. On the other hand, it is pointed out that young Nepalese from the hills who join the British Army as Gurkhas are very quick to learn how to handle and service complicated weapons and electronic equipment, and that there is no reason to suppose that if given the proper training and motivation they would be any less quick to pick up industrial skills as well.

There is no doubt that the key to Nepal's future is connected with, as much as anything, the country's foreign relations. Foreign aid has been decisive in the development of Nepal, and it is remarkable just how many countries have contributed. A recent estimate indicates that in the period from 1952 to 1967 the United States gave Nepal about $100 million in aid, while during the same period India gave over $71 million, China over $18 million and Russia over $20 million. In addition, a large variety of other countries gave the Nepalese over 9 million dollars. (India, China and the United States, in that order, are now the largest donors.) Most of these countries have some sort of political ax to grind in the area—with at least one notable exception: the Swiss. It is difficult to imagine any possible political motivation for Swiss aid in Nepal, and yet the Swiss have one of the most effective, if small-scale, programs in the country.

The Swiss interest in Nepal goes back to the early 1950s, when, at the invitation of the government, the well-known Swiss geologist and explorer Tony Hagen began a series of geological studies of the country that lasted some seven years. Hagen, accompanied by a few Sherpas, walked thousands of miles in Nepal and probably came to know the country better than any Westerner—and perhaps any Nepali—before or since. Most of the places that he visited are now closed to foreigners, so it is unlikely that there will be another series of explorations like Hagen's for a long time to come. Hagen wrote an excellent book, with superb photographs, on Nepal and concluded that rural Nepalese need three things urgently: suspension bridges, hospitals and doctors, and schools. Perhaps because of Tony Hagen's work and writings and because of the Swiss alpine expeditions to Nepal, the Swiss have an especially fond relationship with this country whose geographical problems they find so similar to their own. They have built bridges in rural Nepal; and in Jiri, in the east, they have set up a sort of model village with a hospital clinic. Moreover, the Swiss introduced modern dairy farming to the country. In 1955, with financial support from New Zealand, another country that has had a close and disinterested relation with Nepal—probably because of Sir Edmund Hillary—the Swiss set up a cheese plant in Langtang, six days' walk from Kathmandu. Now there are several cheese factories in the country, and cheese and butter made from yak's milk (yak cheese is, by the way, delicious) have become an important export.

In 1950, when the Chinese moved into Tibet, a massive flow of refugees began pouring into Nepal, Bhutan, Sikkim and India. There are now about eight thousand Tibetan refugees left in Nepal out of the original group of fifteen thousand, and the Swiss have made very important contributions to their resettlement. (A small number have even gone to Switzerland to live.) Outside Kathmandu, in Jawalakhel, there is a large refugee village under the general supervision of the Swiss aid program. Most of these Tibetans work at rug weaving. A Tibetan rug is a work of art. Made of thick, brightly colored wool, it is resplendent in traditional decorations of dragons and the like. There is a sort of rug factory in Jawalakhel run by Tibetans who chant in unison while they weave. When I visited it, there was a certain amount of gloom because, due to the Middle East War and the blockage of the Suez Canal, rug shipments to Europe had been temporarily curtailed and the factory was going through a serious economic crisis.

While in Kathmandu, I had the chance to meet one of the real authorities on Tibet and Tibetan life—an Austrian-born alpinist named Peter Aufschnaiter, leader of the German expedition to Nanga Parbat, in Pakistan, in 1939. He was interned in India by the British as an enemy alien and escaped to Tibet with Heinrich Harrer, who later wrote *Seven Years in Tibet* based on their experience. Aufschnaiter, who is now a citizen of Nepal living near Kathmandu and working in the development of electric power, remained in Tibet even after Harrer had left, and finally escaped just in front of the advancing Chinese. He is a very shy man, with immense personal charm and a deep love of the Tibetans. I asked him how the life of the Tibetans in Nepal compared with what it had been in Tibet. He said that, materially, it was better now; the Tibetans have medical clinics and schools that they never had before. But he thought that they were less happy. He said that in Tibet they had had an easygoing life with a great deal of time left over for the arts, dancing and religious celebrations, while now they have to work very hard to make a living.

Apart from the great powers, and the Swiss, many other countries have programs in Nepal. The British have set up radio broadcasting facilities and built roads, the West Germans have helped to establish a technical institute, the Australians have contributed to improving the water supply, the Japanese have been helping in hydroelectric-power development, the Canadians furnished wheat to Nepal when there were food shortages, there are Nepalese studying in Poland, the French have just opened up an embassy in Kathmandu and have been helping with the development of the Nepalese tourist industry, and the Yugoslavs and Bulgarians have entered into trade agreements with Nepal.

An interesting case is that of the Israelis. Contacts between Nepal and Israel go back to 1959, when the then Nepalese Prime Minister B. P. Koirala accepted an invitation to visit Israel. Shortly after his visit Koirala was swept from power by the King, and for a year or so contacts between Israel and Nepal were broken off. But in 1960 the King decided, despite Arab pressures, to open diplomatic relations with Israel, which he visited in the autumn of 1963. From 1962 to the present, Israel has financed the studies of many Nepalese students in that country and has been cooperating with the Nepalese in construction projects. Most recently the Israelis helped to train a Nepalese Army paratroop brigade. One consequence of this for the Israelis is that Nepal has followed a generally moderate and friendly line in the United Nations, unlike her neighbors India and Pakistan, who have sided with the Arabs. Social developments in Israel, especially the kibbutzim, appear to have captured the imagination of some of the young Nepalese. I met a young man in Kathmandu who told me that he was engaged in a program to start kibbutzim in rural Nepal. When I questioned him a bit more closely it turned out that what he really meant was that he was helping to set up cooperatively owned stores in the countryside that would compete with the privately owned stores and thus keep the prices down.

But the name *kibbutz* had somehow stuck in his imagination and as far as he was concerned he was constructing *kibbutzim*.

In many ways Nepal's future depends on how it can maintain balance and independence with respect to its two giant and mutually hostile neighbors, China and India. Since the British left India, India's relationship with Nepal has gone through considerable evolution. The Nepalese have a long tradition of political independence, and Nepal's foreign policy with respect to India has been an attempt to establish its independence while, at the same time, having to face the political and economic reality of Indian power. (There is one curious manifestation of Nepalese independence—the time is ten minutes later in Nepal than in India since the sun gets to Kathmandu ten minutes earlier than it does to New Delhi. India has only one time—that of New Delhi. The Nepalese also regard Saturday as the day of rest while both the Indians and Pakistanis take Sunday.) Nepal's only outlet to the sea is through India, a fact that apparently inspired Nehru to state during the early 1950s, "We recognise Nepal as an independent country and wish her well. But even a child knows that one cannot go to Nepal without passing through India." This may have been true in 1950, but now a child can go by air to Kathmandu from Dacca or Bangkok (to be sure, with India's permission to overfly its territory), and if one is so disposed, one can come down from Tibet on the "Chinese Road." For India, Nepal represents five hundred miles of strategic mountain frontier, since once the Himalayas have been crossed in Nepal, the country merges into northern India with no natural barriers. The Indians have had check posts in northern Nepal for some time. When I visited Namche Bazar, near Mount Everest, I met a few Indians who were running a wireless station in Namche. In 1955 King Mahendra invited the Chinese ambassador to India to visit him in Kathmandu. This marked a turning point in Nepal's relations with India and China and the beginning of Mahendra's attempt to balance off the influence of the two countries for the benefit of Nepal. In 1956 Nepal signed its first aid agreement with China, and in January of 1957 Chou En-lai paid a state visit to Kathmandu. In 1962 Nepal's relations with her neighbors took a dramatic turn when India and China went to war. It then became of crucial importance to India that its relations with Nepal be solid and cordial. There had previously been a good deal of friction between the two countries over tariff questions and, above all, over the fact that the Nepali Congress Party had mounted raids against the government of the King from northern India. But, with the Chinese at their doorstep, the Indians quickly moved to end all of the sources of tension with the Nepalese. (In particular they stopped the Congress raids.) King Mahendra, for his part, had already gone to Peking and concluded the agreement with the Chinese that led to the construction of the road from Kathmandu to the Tibetan border.

At present, Nepal maintains a strict official neutrality as between the two countries. There have been guerrilla incidents on Nepal's borders with Tibet, provoked by the so-called Khampas, refugees from the Kham province of Tibet, who were, in some cases, former members of the Dalai Lama's army. Much of this activity has taken place around the ancient kingdom of Mustang, in the northwest part of the country—in fact, north of the Himalayas, on the Tibetan plateau. Mustang was, until recently, an independent, rarely visited principality loosely associated with Nepal, but it is now part of the kingdom. It is not clear whether the Khampa raids are simple acts of brigandy or are politically motivated, or both. (Some people have claimed that the Khampas were being supported by the Nationalist Chinese.) In any case, they have been a source of embarrassment to the Nepalese government, which has taken steps to stop them, including closing Mustang to all foreign visitors.

India's concern with China has given the Nepalese a certain room for diplomatic maneuvering, but it is still true that Nepal is extremely dependent on India economically. Since 1962, Indian currency has no longer been legal tender in Nepal, but the two countries are so closely tied economically that shortly after India devalued the rupee in 1966, a year or so later, and presumably as a direct consequence, Nepal followed. Whatever the government's attitude may be, it is quite clear to anyone who looks into the matter that the Nepalese "man in the street" has some, if not a good deal of, distrust of the Chinese. In the north this suspicion appears to be on religious grounds. The first thing that the Chinese did in Tibet was to destroy the monasteries that were at the heart of Buddhist religious life there. Those Nepalese who are Buddhist learned a sharp lesson from this and do not want to see the same thing happen to them. Among the Hindus, in the south, the attitudes are more complex. Their religious orientation is toward India, and many Hindu Nepalese that I talked to seem to have attitudes about the Chinese that border on race prejudice. On several occasions people in Kathmandu told me that they did not like the Chinese, because they ate monkeys and snakes. There are Chinese in Kathmandu, where the Chinese

Embassy is, and they often appear in silent knots, dressed in blue Mao uniforms, in the local bazaars. At one time the Chinese were giving away Mao buttons, but the government of Nepal objected and then provided Mahendra buttons for the Nepalese people, who like to wear buttons and decorations so long as they are brightly colored. There are a few bookstores in Kathmandu that sell the latest works from Peking, including a book on Chinese mountain climbing in which it is claimed that the Chinese climbed Mount Everest at night and planted a bust of Mao at the summit. (Most climbers who know Everest doubt that this is true, although they say that the Chinese do have outstanding climbers and have done some very difficult climbs in the Himalayas.) The Chinese in Kathmandu stay pretty much to themselves, and no one is really sure what their thoughts are about the future of Nepal. However, most people doubt that the Chinese are interested in taking over the country by force, for this would involve a large-scale war with India that the Chinese appear to want to avoid. In this respect there is a story, perhaps apocryphal, that made the rounds in Kathmandu. An American is supposed to have asked King Mahendra what he would do if the Chinese sent tanks down the road from Tibet. The King is said to have answered, "I would inform you."

The future of Nepal is very much tied to the strength and wisdom of the King and his relation to the people. The Nepalese people are honest, attractive, resourceful and good-humored. Although it may sound romantic, it is true that they sing while they work. They sing in the fields and they sing when they carry loads up and down the countryside on their backs. They have lived for a long time in repression and ignorance, but, with modern communications and the ever-increasing presence of tourists from the West, they are becoming more and more aware of the potentialities of life. Some people who visit Nepal are somewhat appalled by what they regard as a loss of innocence—the replacement of the old village culture, with all its joys, sorrows and beauties, by the transistor radio and the cement building. But one must understand that it is the Nepalese people who have chosen the road to development. They desperately want to enter the modern world, and they will do so, whatever anyone else may think about it. At the moment, the King is in full control of the country. He is genuinely loved by the people, who, even when they criticize the government, do so in a way that exempts the King. If the King is to continue to remain above criticism—and there are recent indications from Nepal that this may no longer be the case—then the villagers and townspeople must begin to realize their newly awakened hopes and visions of a better life. No individual, and no nation either, can live indefinitely on unfulfilled expectations.

One of the more than 2,000 pagoda
temples in the Kathmandu Valley.

Religious monuments, both Buddhist and Hindu, cover the hill where the shrine of Swayambhunath stands, near Kathmandu.

Newar wood carving embroiders the windows of Kathmandu. ▶

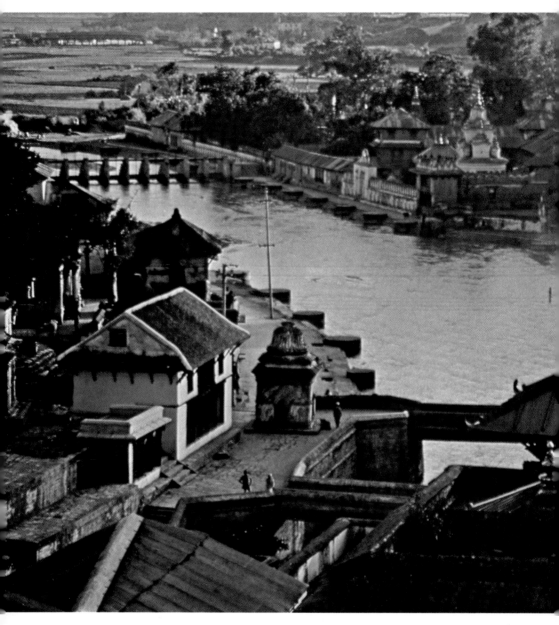

The Bagamati River, where the dead are buried in Kathmandu.

Religious carvings at Swayambhu-▶
nath: a *dorge*, symbolic lightning bolt,
at left, and a demon figure.

Mixed motifs: street scene in Kathmandu.

A barber plies his trade in the open
air in downtown Kathmandu.

A Tibetan porter with the face of a prince.

A lama in northern Nepal, who told us he was going blind; ▶
some of our Tamang porters, far from their homes in the hills of
Kathmandu, look on.

Prayer flags crown a high point on a Himalayan trail.

A lama and his Tibetan dance masks at the monastery in Thyangboche, near Everest.

A musician of western Nepal. ▶

We have pitched our tents on the grounds of a monastery in northern Nepal, just in front of a small stupa under Buddha's ever watchful eyes.

◀Rocks and slabs filled with religious carvings, which add to one's *sönam* (the measure of credit which a Buddhist hopes to accumulate in his present life in order to escape the pain of rebirth).

Fortune has wings: a child in rural Nepal. ▶

A farmhouse in western Nepal, with the Annapurna massif in the distance.

The cigarette is the consolation and perhaps the curse of the Nepalese. These children are twelve and thirteen years old.

Wheeled vehicles are rare in the Nepalese countryside. The
only wheels one sees there are water wheels, prayer wheels
and carousels like these built for children.

Sherpas in front of a school founded by Sir Edmund Hillary in northern Nepal.

Sherpa children; half of all such youngsters die before they reach fifteen years of age.

Most bridges in Nepal consist of a few logs and will be swept away by the annual monsoon. All local commerce in the hill country is borne on human backs over these log bridges.

This bridge, one of the sturdiest we found in rural Nepal, links the main trails connecting Kathmandu and the Himalayas.

Our porters make their way down a ▶ small ladder joining terraced fields in typical scrub jungle farmland in rural Nepal.

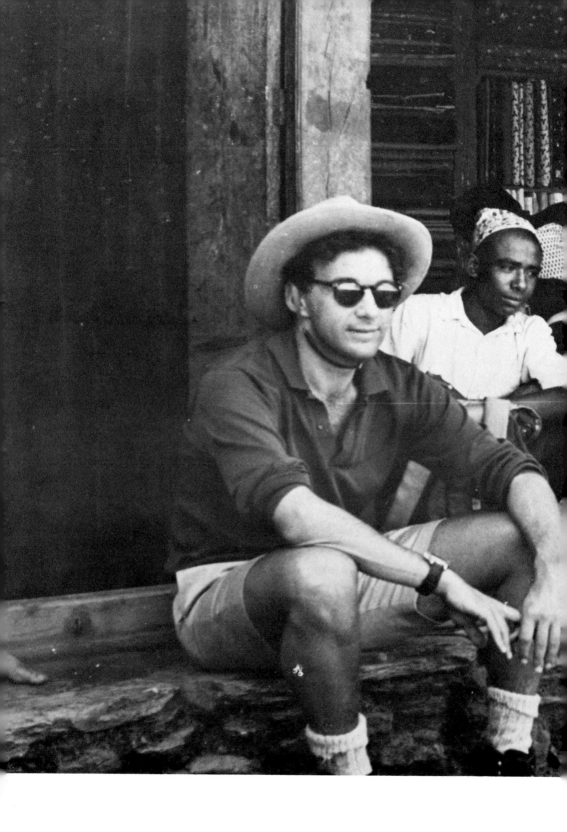

On the first day of our trek to Everest, I take a rest from the fierce sun at a small boutique.

◀Ang Dorge and the "yeti" scalp.

Our party on Everest, two miles below the peak.

Bazaar day in Namche Bazar, the district capital of Khumbu, ▶
high up in Sherpa country.

Michèle and I discuss the wireless situation with young Sub-
Inspector Rana (right). The Sub-Inspector's garden, seen behind us, was consumed by a yak soon after.

Michèle Jaccoux after several days on the trail.

3
Some Walk-Going

*I*n many ways, Ila Tsering, who is thirty-five, is a typical Sherpa. Like most of his fellow tribesmen, he is, by geographic nationality, a Nepalese. Like all Sherpas, he is short (five feet three, the Nepalese average), dark and Mongolian-looking. (In Tibetan, "Sherpa" means "man from the east," but no one knows what "the east" refers to, exactly. Several centuries ago, it is thought, the Sherpa tribe migrated south into Nepal and northern India from Tibet. As for the Tibetans themselves, they look astonishingly like our American Indians.) Like most Sherpas, he wears his hair short. (Tibetans wear *their* hair extremely long, like a woman's, and tie it up in coils with bright ribbons.) Like most Sherpas, he is married to one woman (both polygamy and polyandry, though now forbidden by Nepalese law, are practiced by a few Sherpas, the most common arrangement being the marriage of a woman to two brothers) and has a fairly large family—three boys and a girl. As is true of many Sherpa families, there is a history of tuberculosis in Ila's family—his wife had the disease until it was arrested by the recent arrival of modern medicine in his community. Like most Sherpas, Ila lives in the Solu-Khumbu region of Nepal. Solu and Khumbu are contiguous districts in the northeast, next to Mount Everest. Solu, the more southerly, is in the "lowlands"—its villages are at about nine thousand feet. In Khumbu, the villages are at eleven or twelve thousand feet, and the yak pastures, where the Sherpa herdsmen live in the summer, are as high as seventeen thousand feet, which is almost two thousand feet higher than Mont Blanc, the highest mountain in Europe. Ila and his family live in Namche Bazar, the district capital of Khumbu, which is at twelve thousand feet. Like most Sherpas, Ila is multilingual. His mother tongue, Sherpa, is closely related to Tibetan but has no written form, so Tibetan serves as the written language. Ila speaks and writes Tibetan. He also speaks and writes Nepali. Most Sherpas now understand Nepali, and the younger generation, having had the advantage of formal schooling, read and write it as well. In addition, Ila speaks Hindustani, a mixture of Hindi and Urdu spoken in India. He understands English and speaks it with both a charming accent and a rather astonishing turn of phrase. (There does not seem to be any sound in Sherpa equivalent to the English "f," so "fruit" comes out "prut" and "breakfast" "birkpass.") Like all Sherpas, Ila is a Lamaistic Buddhist, his religious life being guided by the lamas who live and study in the monasteries in Solu-Khumbu. The spiritual leader of the Lamaistic Buddhists is the Dalai Lama, who lived in Lhasa before the Chinese occupation of Tibet. He is now in India, and for the Sherpas of Khumbu his spiritual representative is the abbot of the monastery at Thyangboche, a few miles from Namche Bazar. In addition, the Sherpas are animists—they believe in a complex set of spirits and deities who live in the streams, trees and high mountains of Solu-Khumbu.

What distinguishes Ila from most Sherpas, who are farmers, herdsmen or traders, is his occupation, which he describes as "some walk-going." Before 1965, when the government temporarily banned all mountaineering expeditions because their number had become unmanageable, along with their irresponsibility (they would go where they had no permission to go, and, more important, several of them actually crossed the border into Tibet, inflaming the Chinese government), Ila's "walk-going" took him with English, Japanese, Indian and American climbing teams. His function was what he calls "carrying go." There is carrying and there is carrying; Ila's version consisted of transporting food and other supplies to very high altitudes over difficult mountain terrain. Technically, Ila is a "tiger." The British, who discovered the extraordinary physical and human virtues of the Sherpas in the course of their first Everest expeditions, in the 1920s, gave the nickname "tiger" to those Sherpas who carried the highest or who showed special courage. It soon became a custom for the Himalayan Club of Darjeeling—the Indian hill station east of Nepal where many early assaults on the peaks were mounted—to make formal "tiger" awards to outstanding Sherpas. In the 1950s, a Himalayan Society was formed in Nepal and became a kind of Sherpa union. (It was temporarily dissolved in 1965 when the ban on climbing was imposed, and then revived in 1969 when the ban was lifted.) Every Sherpa registered with the society still has a sort of passport bearing his picture and his signature—a thumbprint if he can't write—along with a record of his work with various expeditions. The Himalayan Society also set the rates for "carrying," which are now somewhere between ten and fifteen Nepalese rupees—a dollar to a dollar and a half—a day. By Nepalese standards, this is very good pay. Ila has been with many expeditions throughout the Himalayas, but his most outstanding work was probably done with the American expedition to Mount Everest in 1963. On March 23rd of that year, he was with a group that was caught in an avalanche on the lower slopes of Everest; an American climber, Jake Breitenbach, was killed, and a Sherpa, Ang Pema, was badly injured. Ila carried Ang Pema down to the base camp on his back. There the members of the expedition debated whether or not to continue, and decided to go on. The success of the expedition was due, at least in part, to the fact that the Sherpas were willing to carry on after the accident. On May 1st, James Whittaker and a Sherpa, Nawang Gombu, of Darjeeling, made it to the top. On May 21st, Ila and four other Sherpas carried to an altitude of 27,250 feet on the West Ridge of Everest—less than two thousand feet below the summit and higher than all but a handful of mountains in the world—in support of two successful American assaults, each by a different route. For his work on Everest (before the final push, Ila is reported to have said, "All smart Sherpas down sick. Only crazy Sherpas up here"), Ila was selected—along with four other

Sherpas, two from Solu-Khumbu and two from Darjeeling—to visit the United States, with the aid of a grant from the State Department's Bureau of Educational and Cultural Affairs. On the way, Ila stopped in Switzerland long enough to climb the Matterhorn, which he found pretty tame. On July 8th, President Kennedy presented the Hubbard Medal of the National Geographic Society to the American members of the expedition and to the Sherpas as well. Hanging in Ila's house in Namche Bazar is a delightful picture showing the late President bending down to put the medal's ribbon around Ila's neck. Both men are grinning broadly.

After 1965, the expedition Sherpas of Solu-Khumbu fell on relatively hard times, because there was no expeditionary work for them. Their situation would have been incomparably worse if it were not for a retired British Army officer, Lieutenant-Colonel James Owen Merion Roberts, formerly of 2d King Edward VII's Own Gurkha Rifles. Roberts, who is now fifty-three, has been climbing in the Himalayas for more than thirty years, and served as the transportation officer for the 1963 American Everest expedition. (This was no sinecure, since the expedition required nine hundred porters to move its equipment from Kathmandu to the base of Everest, a distance of more than two hundred miles through some of the most rugged terrain on earth.) There is probably no one in the world who knows the Himalayas better than Roberts; in addition, he served as military attaché to the British Embassy in Kathmandu from 1958 to 1961, which has given him considerable familiarity with the intricacies of Nepalese governmental administration. He speaks both Nepali and Hindustani, and is a brilliant mountain photographer. In 1965, Roberts, who lives in Kathmandu, founded an outfit called Mountain Travel. His idea was to organize and outfit small trekking expeditions into the back country of Nepal—which is completely inaccessible except on foot—for people who were willing to hike and camp but might not know how to get along in a strange, primitive country with an incomprehensible language. His first clients were three American ladies, aged fifty-six, sixty-two and sixty-four, from the Midwest. They must have been in splendid shape, because, in the company of three Sherpas and nine porters, all supplied by Roberts, they made the trek from Kathmandu to Namche Bazar and back—a dog-leg route of 190 miles each way as the crow flies—in a little over a month, and apparently enjoyed the trip thoroughly. (The distance as seen by a crow is not a very relevant measure of this trip, since so much of it is nearly vertical; some of the passes rise to

nearly twelve thousand feet.) Today, Roberts handles several hundred trekkers a year and employs the equivalent of three or four major expeditions'
worth of Sherpas as guides and cooks, and at least a hundred and fifty
porters, who are recruited from the hill towns along the way. For a fee that
comes to a little more than eleven dollars a day per person for the Everest
trek—which, if one goes all the way to the base of Everest, several days'
march beyond Namche, lasts thirty-seven days, round trip—Roberts supplies food, tents and sleeping bags, along with sufficient personnel to carry
the equipment and cook the food. All the trekker must supply is his personal gear and what Roberts calls in one of his brochures "Feet in good,
hard shape."

Ila Tsering is one of Colonel Roberts' *sirdars*, or expedition leaders. It
was in this capacity that I came to know him. He was the *sirdar* for a thirty-
five-day trek that I made with my friends Claude and Michèle Jaccoux
(he is a French alpine guide, and she is a former member of the French
national ski team and is now a ski instructor) into the high mountain country of Solu-Khumbu in fulfillment of a childhood dream—to see Mount
Everest. Its history and the almost legendary tales surrounding the attempts
to climb it have always fascinated me. Mount Everest is a "British mountain," thanks to Edmund Hillary and Tenzing Norkay in 1953, although the
British were nearly forestalled by two Swiss expeditions in 1952. (And if
the British had failed in 1953, an extremely strong French group had been
granted permission by the Nepalese government to make an attempt in
1954.) Until 1950, almost no foreigners were allowed in; when that ban was
lifted, the government started selling climbing rights to its mountains, which
include eight of the ten highest in the world. The fee was arranged according to altitude. Up to 1965, when all climbing was temporarily banned,
the eight highest—Everest (29,028), Kanchenjunga (28,146), Lhotse
(27,980), Makalu (27,750), Dhaulagiri (26,811), Cho-oyu (26,750), Mansalu (26,658), and Annapurna (26,504)—cost 4,800 Nepalese rupees, or
about $700, apiece. Any other mountains above 25,000 feet cost 3,200
rupees each, and mountains below 25,000 feet cost 1,600—a bit less than
$250. (The last category must have presented some ambiguities of interpre-
tation, because northern Nepal abounds in "hills" and glacial passes that
range between 18,000 and 20,000 feet but, in their context, hardly seem like
real mountains at all. Although all of the "eight-thousanders"—the peaks
over 8,000 meters, or about 26,250 feet—have been climbed, most of the

mountains in Nepal have never been attempted, and a vast number of them are not even named.) In 1969 the Nepalese government lifted the climbing ban imposed in 1965, and at the same time it raised the rates somewhat. The going rates are $1,000 for Everest (the Japanese are scheduled to try a new route on the South Face of Everest in 1971), $800 for other peaks over 26,000 feet, and $600 for peaks below 26,000 feet.

In any event, it was the British who "discovered" Mount Everest. In 1852 —according, at least, to the legend—a Bengali, Radhanath Sikhdar, who was working as a statistician for the British Survey of India is said to have rushed into the office of Sir Andrew Waugh, the Surveyor General, and announced, "Sir, I have discovered the highest mountain in the world!" Until that time, the mountain in question had been listed in the survey as "Peak XV," with no altitude shown. It was not until 1865 that Sir Andrew formally named it for his predecessor, Sir George Everest. The first altitude given for the peak, in 1852, was 29,002 feet; on the basis of later measurements (in 1907 and 1921–22), this was raised to 29,145 feet; and it has now shrunk back to 29,028 feet as the result of a survey made in 1955 under the auspices of the Indian government. Erosion, no doubt; reduces the height of the mountain, and there is reason to believe that the geological forces that raised the Himalayas from the sea in the first place are still at work, but these forces work rather slowly, and the discrepancies in Everest's altitude over the past century are certainly attributable to errors in measurement.*

Of course, the Tibetans and Sherpas who lived near the base of Everest were aware of its existence long before the British arrived in India. Indeed, the Tibetan name for Everest is Chomo-lungma, which has been translated as "Goddess Mother of the World" or "Goddess Mother of the Snows." But big as it is, Everest is one of the most difficult mountains in the world

---

* Dr. B. L. Gulatee, director of the 1955 survey, commented in *The Himalayan Journal*, a publication devoted to Himalayan exploration: "The new determination stands in a class by itself, and its close agreement with the older [1852] value does not signify that the latter was well determined. It is really due to the fact that like is not being compared with like. Judged by modern standards, the earlier deduction of the height of Mount Everest was vague in several respects, and was burdened with large errors on account of neglect or incomplete consideration of certain physical factors. It so happened that by chance the various individual errors, although large, have tended to cancel each other."

to get a good view of. From the Kathmandu Valley it is not visible at all, although one can see it on a clear day from various hilly vantage points a short drive from the valley. Yet even then it does not seem like much; indeed, if one does not know just where to look one can easily miss it altogether. It is no wonder that the Nepalese thought several other peaks were higher. (In some books on Nepal written before 1850, Dhaulagiri, in western Nepal, was said to be the highest mountain in the world.) Because Nepal was completely closed to expeditions before 1950, the southern flank of the mountain, which lies in Nepal, remained unexplored until it was visited briefly in that year by a small British-American party. As for the northern approaches to the peak, Tibet too was closed to Westerners during the nineteenth century, but in 1904 Sir Francis Younghusband arrived with a contingent of British troops and opened up diplomatic and trade relations with the country. Still, it was not until 1921 that a British reconnaisance party made its way to the Rongbuk Valley, at the northern base of the mountain. In 1922 and 1924, British parties engaged in two absolutely extraordinary attempts to climb the mountain from the Tibetan side. A member of both parties was George Leigh-Mallory. (It was Mallory who, at a lecture in Philadelphia, replied "Because it is there" to a question about why he wanted to climb Everest.) Since first coming to Everest, in 1921, Mallory had become enslaved by the mountain. E. F. Norton, a climber with the 1924 party, wrote of him: "The conquest of the mountain became an obsession with him, and for weeks and months he devoted his whole time and energy to it, incessantly working at plans and details of organization; and when it came to business he expended on it every ounce of his unrivalled physical energy."

Reading the accounts of these pioneering attempts, one is constantly struck by the almost completely casual and innocent heroism of the participants. Almost all were public-school men (Mallory, indeed, taught at Charterhouse), and, when not otherwise occupied, could be found in small tents at various altitudes reading aloud to one another from *The Spirit of Man*, *Hamlet* or *King Lear*. As Mallory wrote in his account of the 1922 expedition, "On another occasion, I had the good fortune to open my Shakespeare at the very place where Hamlet addresses the ghost. 'Angels and Ministers of Grace defend us,' I began, and the theme was so congenial that we stumbled on enthusiastically, reading the parts in turn through half the play." This reading of the Bard took place at 21,000 feet, above the Rongbuk Glacier, and shortly thereafter Mallory and a companion, without oxygen, managed to climb to 27,000 feet—just 2,000 feet short of the summit. A second team, using oxygen, got a little higher, but a third attempt on the peak ended in disaster when seven Sherpas were killed in an avalanche. This expedition marked the first use of oxygen (which the Sherpas called "English air") in climbing, and it also marked the first appearance of Sherpas in a mountaineering expedition. In 1924, the British were back en masse, with 350 porters and twelve climbers. Mallory was now thirty-seven, which seems to be a prime age for Himalayan climbing. (Young climbers usually lack the kind of temperament required to slog away day after day, often with little or no progress, on a Himalayan giant.) On June 4th, E. F. Norton and T. H. Somervell reached over 28,000 feet, without oxygen. On June 7th, Mallory started up with a young companion, Andrew Irvine. They were followed by N. E. Odell, the expedition geologist (who, incidentally, discovered marine fossils high on the mountain, showing its suboceanic origins). Odell had not come on the expedition primarily as a climber, but in the early stages he had shown himself to be so strong that he had been given the task of following Mallory and Irvine, one camp behind, to offer them whatever support they needed. On the 7th, Odell, who was in Camp V, at a little over 25,000 feet, received a note from Mallory carried down from Camp VI by some Sherpas, which ended, "Perfect weather for the job!" The next morning, Odell started up after Mallory and Irvine, and his record of what he saw remains one of the most celebrated passages in all alpine literature:

At about 26,000 feet, I climbed a little crag, which could possibly have been circumvented but which I decided to tackle direct, more perhaps as a test of my condition than for any other reason. There was scarcely 100 feet of it, and as I reached the top there was a sudden clearing of the atmosphere above me, and I saw the whole summit ridge and final peak of Everest unveiled. I noticed far away, on a snow slope leading up to what seemed to me to be the last step but one from the base of the final pyramid, a tiny object moving and approaching the rock step. A second object followed, and then the first climbed to the top of the step. As I stood intently watching this dramatic appearance, the scene became enveloped in cloud once more. . . .

This was the last time that Mallory and Irvine were ever seen. Odell continued up alone—and in a driving blizzard—to over 27,000 feet in the vain hope of finding them. But there was no trace. Nine years later, on the next expedition to the mountain, Mallory's ice ax was recovered at a point not far above the place from which Odell had been watching. How did it get there? Did the men get to the top and fall on the descent, or were they lost in the snows before reaching the summit? No one will ever know.

In the 1930's, the British mounted four Everest expeditions from Tibet, the last one in 1938. All were stopped a thousand feet or so from the summit. In 1933, they sent two small planes over the summit of Everest, and for the first time the Nepalese approaches to the mountain were photographed. In 1934, a rather bizarre and somewhat pathetic English mystic named Maurice Wilson made a solo attempt on the mountain in order to publicize some of his theories, which included the notion that if a man were able to go without food for three weeks he would emerge in a state like that of a newborn child but with the benefit of all the experience of his past life. Wilson had never been on a mountain, but he somehow got the idea that if he could succeed in climbing Everest alone it would help to establish his theories. At first, he planned to crash a small plane as high as possible on the mountain and make the rest of the trip on foot. He got as far as Purnea, in India, where his plane was confiscated, and then walked the rest of the way—about two hundred miles—to Darjeeling. There he trained for four months and arranged with some Sherpas to take him, disguised as a Tibetan, to the base of Everest. He, of course, had no permission to climb, but he made a favorable impression on the head lama of the monastery in Rongbuk, with whom he had many discussions. In May, 1934, he started for the summit and died of exposure in his tent somewhere above 21,000 feet. His body and diary were found by the British expedition of 1935.

Himalayan climbing was suspended during the Second World War, and it was not until 1950 that expeditions to Everest were resumed. (In 1947 there was another solo attempt by a Canadian, E. L. Denman, who also disguised himself as a Tibetan and who was accompanied by none other than Tenzing. They retreated safely from a point a little above where Maurice Wilson had died.) The political situation had completely altered. Tibet was now closed and Nepal open. In 1950 a small Anglo-American group made the first trek by Westerners into Namche Bazar, and in 1951 a very strong group led by the great Himalayan climber Eric Shipton and including Hillary set out from Dharan, in eastern Nepal, and explored the whole southern flank of Everest, mapping the general outlines of what became the climbing route up the South Face. The next year, the Swiss got permission to try the mountain and again approached it via Namche Bazar. The party succeeded in forcing the great ice fall that leads from the Khumbu Glacier to the Western Cwm, a glacial valley that Mallory had seen from the north in 1921 and had given a Welsh name in honor of the fact that he had done his first climbing in Wales. In late May, Tenzing and Raymond Lambert, a famous Swiss guide from Geneva, reached a point on the South Face that was a little more than a thousand feet below the summit. The Swiss were back in the fall of 1952, and once again Tenzing and Lambert were stopped at about the same point. Of course, on May 29, 1953, Hillary and Tenzing reached the top, following the Swiss route as far as it went, and in the snows of the summit Tenzing buried a little red-and-blue pencil, given him by his daughter Nima, as an offering to Chomo-lungma, the Goddess Mother. This was Tenzing's seventh Everest expedition.

Ever since the Swiss traversed Nepal from Kathmandu to Namche Bazar, all expeditions to Everest have used substantially the same route, and have set up their camps at more or less the same places. Indeed, all of Roberts' Everest trekkers use the Swiss route. This is very convenient, since the Swiss published an extensive account of their trip across Nepal in a book called *Avant-Premières à l'Everest*, from which the prospective trekker can get an idea of what he is up against. In reading the book while my trip with Claude and Michèle Jaccoux was still in the formative stages, I was immediately struck by the decisive role of the monsoon in determining when one can travel in Nepal. The monsoon comes to Nepal in early June and leaves, as a rule, by mid-September. It is caused by the fact that during the early summer the thin, dry air above the Tibetan plain becomes heated and rises, creating an enormous low-pressure system to the north of Nepal that draws up moist air from the Bay of Bengal. This moist air is wrung dry as it rises to cross the Himalayan barrier, with the result that to the north of the mountains the land is essentially a desert, while to the south it is something of a tropical paradise. During the monsoon, travel is all but impossible. The dirt trails, often exceedingly steep, become as slippery as ice, and the rivers are swollen with rain and with water from the melting snows of the Himalayas. On the trek from Kathmandu to Namche there are innumerable rivers to be crossed, and the bridges, if they exist at all, generally consist of a few logs thrown across the stream. Everest is to the east of Kathmandu, and all east–west travel in Nepal involves crossing the innumerable rivers that flow south from Tibet. During the monsoon, the logs are carried away, and the bridge has to be rebuilt the following fall; it is quite rare to find a bridge that is high enough and strong enough to resist the monsoon waters. A third difficulty of travel during the monsoon is the insects, snakes and, above all, leeches which abound in the tropical countryside during the summer. While a leech bite does not usually cause any serious trouble, there is nothing more revolting. The leeches of Nepal are, on the average, about an inch long. After a rain, they line the foliage along a muddy trail and sway back and forth until a man or an animal passes. Sometimes they drop down from leaves above the trail, but most often they climb into one's shoes, and lodge themselves between one's toes. It is useless, and even somewhat dangerous, to pull a leech off, since this causes a wound that tends to ulcerate. As a rule, leech bites do not hurt, so one is unaware of having been bitten until one discovers that one's clothes are covered with blood. Traveling over leech-infested terrain is no picnic.

All Everest expeditions have had to reckon with the monsoon. There are two possible strategies: to arrive at the base of the mountain in the late spring and climb until the monsoon strikes, or to arrive in the fall just after the monsoon and climb until the winter snows set in, during late November. In 1952 the Swiss tried both, and after reading their account of the trek to Everest in the early fall, before the monsoon had blown itself out— Lambert severely sprained his ankle when he slipped on a wet trail, and the leader of the expedition, Dr. Gabriel Chevalley, acquired a seriously infected ankle from a leech bite—I decided that, whatever else, we should avoid the bad weather. What with one thing and another, the earliest we could make the trek was in late September, a timing that worked out very well for Jaccoux, since it fell exactly between his climbing and his skiing seasons. Sometime in April I wrote to Roberts, and a few weeks later I got back a cheerful, businesslike reply on Mountain Travel stationery, which has printed across the bottom "Pack a suitcase and take off for Mount Everest"—rather as if it were like a stroll in the park. Roberts indicated that a trek to Everest might well be organized for late September, when, with luck, the monsoon would have ended. These days, Roberts is booked up months in advance, so, monsoon or no, we accepted the dates he proposed and began making arrangements for the trip.

Among other things, Roberts sends his clients a detailed list of things to bring and medical precautions to take. Among the latter is a formidable set of suggested vaccinations, including typhoid, tetanus, cholera, typhus, smallpox, polio, and gamma globulin, to prevent hepatitis. During the spring, I involved myself in all but endless series of visits to my doctor for shots, and I assumed, naïvely, that the Jaccoux were likewise engaged. The French, although they invented vaccination, do not much believe in it, and when I arrived in Europe, in early June, the Jaccoux announced that they were going to take the bare legal minimum—cholera and smallpox—and *tant pis pour les autres*. Despite my fervent arguments about the terrible dangers they were exposing themselves to, they stuck to their intentions, and, I must confess, got through the trek in splendid health. However, they did pay a visit to Dr. Guy de Haynin, the chief surgeon at the hospital at Mulhouse, who had been the expedition doctor for one of the last French expeditions to Nepal and, the summer before, had been the doctor for a French expedition to the Peruvian Andes of which Jaccoux had been a member. In fact, Jaccoux served as de Haynin's medical assistant during the Peruvian expedition. Dr. de Haynin, in a gesture of great kindness, offered to supply us with a complete pharmacy, suitable for every medical situation that we might come up against, short of major surgery. Fortunately, as it turned out, most of the huge array of medicines that we took along came back unused.

Of much more relevance was the matter of clothing. From the Swiss account, it was clear that during the trek the climate was going to change from tropical to arctic. We planned to wind up our trek somewhere near the base camp of the British 1953 Everest expedition, which is at 17,800 feet, and from all accounts we could expect extreme cold, high winds, and snow. On the other hand, during the first week or so of the trek we would be passing through tropical jungles, and our main problem would be avoiding heat prostration. Shorts, bathing suits and parasols would solve the heat and sun problem, but the cold was something else. The Jaccoux teach skiing and, as Michèle said when we were discussing the matter, *"Nous, on connait le froid."* Following their advice and a clothing list supplied by Roberts, I ended up taking along—working from the inside out—long thermal underwear, two wool shirts and a pair of heavy climbing pants, two heavy sweaters, two windproof light nylon jackets, a heavy down jacket, two wool hats, a pair of wool gloves, a pair of leather gloves, a pair of enormous mittens, hiking shoes and climbing shoes, several pairs of extra-heavy wool socks, and a track suit, which Jaccoux had suggested would make a good pair of pajamas. (On one memorable evening when we were camped in our tents in the snow at sixteen thousand feet, I wore almost all of it, and Michèle claimed that she had on seven layers.) In addition, we took three cameras and enough film for several thousand pictures, a portable electric razor, a sewing kit for Michèle, a portable radio (which broke down almost immediately), Malraux's *Anti-mémoires* for Jaccoux, two months' supply of Gauloise cigarettes and an equivalent quantity of pipe tobacco, two decks of cards, two small ice axes and a coil of light nylon climbing rope, and several boxes of laundry soap. I had also purchased twelve aerosol cans of the best Swiss insecticide, and twelve cans of insect repellent, as well as several thousand chlorine tablets for purifying the drinking water. As a last-minute inspiration, we stocked up with vitamin-C tablets, on the ground that there might not be much available in the way of fresh fruit. Actually, we had fruit of one kind or another almost every day.

As it happened, I spent most of that summer near Geneva, which allowed me to undertake an extensive training program of hiking in the Alps. About a month before we were supposed to leave, I slipped on a wet rock during one of these hikes and sprained my ankle, which nearly finished the expedition right then and there. Fortunately, by the time we left, the ankle, although weak, was usable. Jaccoux, on the other hand, was in splendid shape after a summer of guiding, and Michèle, despite a decidedly svelte appearance, has the natural stamina of a musk ox. By early September we had everything in one place, including our visas. Nepal is one of the few countries in the world where one's entry visa does not allow one to travel in the country. Our visas, valid for fourteen days, gave us permission to visit only Kathmandu, Pokhara and Tiger Tops. For our tour, Roberts had had to apply for a "trekking permit" for each of us—a sort of passport, with photograph, which spelled out precisely where we could go. The fact that one is required to have such a document, and the fact that one is not allowed to vary at all from the assigned route, are reflections of the Nepalese government's concern about letting foreigners get too close to its northern border. Under almost no circumstance is a foreigner allowed to get closer than twenty-five miles from Tibet. Even if one charters a plane to see the

Himalayas, the government insists that a representative from the Foreign Ministry be aboard to make sure that the plane does not stray too close. The Nepalese walk a delicate tightrope between China and India, and they are determined not to have their balance disturbed by incidents on the borders. So we filled out long forms for our trekking permits and enclosed several pictures, and in the middle of September Roberts informed us that everything was in order.

By the end of September, Claude and Michèle and I were flying over the flooded rice paddies of northern India, across the Himalayan foothills, past the great snow-covered peaks of western Nepal, and down into the Valley of Kathmandu—surely one of the most spectacular flights in the world. Roberts had sent a Land Rover to meet us at the airport, and later in the day, when we had settled in, he dropped by the hotel to say hello and introduce us to Ila Tsering. Roberts, a courtly, soft-spoken man with a slight limp that apparently does not impede his walking and climbing, has the air of someone who has spent a great deal of his life out of doors. I asked him whether he thought the monsoon was over, and he said that it hadn't rained in two days, which was a good sign. He told us that the leeches had been particularly bad during this monsoon but added, "I shouldn't think you will have much trouble if the rain holds off." While this conversation was going on, Ila stood silent, studying us. I suppose he was wondering what sort of people he was about to spend the next five weeks with. After Roberts left, Ila came to our rooms to see how our equipment was arranged. We had been instructed to have everything packed in plastic bags, which, in turn, were to be put into wicker baskets carried by the porters. Each of us had been allowed about thirty pounds of gear, plus whatever we wanted to carry ourselves. When Ila saw the climbing rope and ice axes, he remarked, "Climbing something?" with a cheerful laugh that seemed to indicate that he didn't take the prospect very seriously.

Early on the morning of September 30th, we piled our gear into one of Roberts' Land Rovers and left Kathmandu on the first lap of the route to Everest. For the first thirty miles, we were able to take advantage of the "Chinese Road." This is an excellent paved road—without a doubt the best in Nepal—built by the Chinese, at the invitation of the Nepalese government, between 1963 and 1967. It runs from a point near Kathmandu to the Tibetan border at Kodari. The road is certainly useful for transporting

people and produce over a rather limited area of Nepal, but the fact that
the Chinese built it so elaborately, and that it leads directly from the capital
city to the Tibetan frontier, has caused a great deal of comment. Foreigners
are allowed to travel only the first sixty miles of it, but for our purposes
only the first thirty-odd miles—to a point called Dolalghat, which is at the
junction of the Indrawatti and Sun Kosi rivers—took us in the direction we
wanted to go. At Dolalghat the rivers are crossed by the Chinese Bridge, a
magnificent structure "just wide enough," as some one has said, "for two
tanks and a motorcycle." The Land Rover let us out in front of an open
shed on the near side of the bridge. Clustered around the shed was a large
assortment of people of various races—Tibetans, Sherpas, Tamangs and
Newars. It took several minutes before it dawned on me that most of them
were connected with our trek. When I finally got them sorted out, our roll
included three Sherpas, in addition to Ila; six Tibetans, who, it later turned
out, were "high-altitude porters," with considerable experience on expeditions and absolutely unbelievable resistance to the cold (among them a
mother and daughter, who, like most Tibetan and Sherpa women, were
capable of carrying almost as much as the men, and who had walked to
Kathmandu from Solu-Khumbu and done a good deal of shopping, the re-
sults of which they were taking back home); and a group of eight or ten
(it varied from day to day) Tamang porters, members of a tribal group
that lives in the high hills near Kathmandu and speaks a Tibeto-Burman
language which is distinct from either Sherpa or Tibetan. The Newars apparently owned the shed, which served as a kind of open-air refreshment
stand. We tried to keep out of the way while Ila began the task of putting
various things of ours into various wicker baskets. There was a total chaos
of people and animals. (It turned out that we were taking along some live
chickens.) For a while we stood in the sun, but it beat down with such a
leaden, tropical intensity that we soon moved into the limited shade afforded
by the shed. Jaccoux had had the inspiration of buying three Indian parasols
in the market the day before, and in addition we had brought along two sun
helmets (Michèle preferred bandannas), all of which were indispensable.
After half an hour or so our caravan was organized, and we crossed the
bridge and started up a nearby trail that turned east, away from the road.

The tone the trek was to take for the next two weeks was set right at
the beginning—up and down. We began at once what Roberts refers to in
his notes for Everest trekkers as "a long and rather tiring climb to over

6,000 feet." To be sure, in comparison with any of the training walks I had taken in the Alps this should have been a bagatelle, and still more so for Jaccoux. But the trail was steep and the heat overbearing. Perspiration streamed down our faces, and at one point, as we passed a little village, Michèle bought a length of cotton cloth, out of which she made a sari to take the place of the jeans she had been wearing. The trail was jammed with people. Almost all commercial transport in rural Nepal is done on human backs, and we saw men, women and children carrying sacks of grain, reams of paper and cloth, long bundles of bamboo poles, salt, and animals too small to be herded. The beginning of our trek coincided with the ten-day Dassain festival, which celebrates the victory of the Goddess Durga over the buffalo-headed demon Mahisasoor. Animals are brought from the countryside to Kathmandu for sacrifice, and many of the animals we saw— chickens, goats and buffaloes—were on their way for that purpose. At one point, I met a man who spoke excellent English and said he was a doctor out on a call in one of the villages—a rare sight in the countryside. The doctor asked where we were going, and when I told him that we were on our way to Namche Bazar and the base of Everest, he looked at me as if I were slightly daft and suggested renting a helicopter.

After walking a couple of hours, we came upon a large pipal tree under which the residents of a nearby village had constructed stone blocks just high enough so that anyone carrying a load could set it down by backing into the block and leaving the basket, or whatever, on the top. It was a delightfully shady spot, and we joined a dozen or so Nepalese who were resting in the shadows. By this time, although we had walked only a few miles, the heat had become so intense that every step in the sun was a major effort, and we were grateful when Ila announced that we would make an early halt and camp close to a spring by some nearby rice fields. We crossed the fields, which were wet and green from the rain of the recent monsoon, and got ready for our first night on the trail. This involved a routine that was maintained for the next five weeks. First, the tents were taken out. We had two light-green ones—one for the Jaccoux and one for me. They were carried by a Tibetan with an extraordinary face, rich with humor and deeply lined. Michèle nicknamed him "l'Indien" because of his remarkable resemblance to an American Indian chief. (The Indian had a marvelous sense of balance, which he demonstrated later by carrying me on his back, like a child, across some thin planks that spanned a monsoon-swollen river. I had started out

on the planks but didn't like their look, and had climbed back to solid
ground. Before I knew what was happening, the Indian had hoisted me on
his back and was trotting across the narrow, swaying boards with the agility
of an acrobat, setting me down gently in the grass on the other side.) At
our nightly camps, there would be a general flurry of activity, usually accompanied by singing, while the tents were rolled out and set up. Another
porter—also a Tibetan, whom Michèle called *"le chanteur"*—always led the
singing, which consisted of some eerie, haunting and terribly sad-sounding
songs of Tibet. Meanwhile, two of the Sherpas, a cook and an assistant
cook—a Roberts' trek has a certain chic—had started a fire to boil water
for tea. At first we had some misgivings about the water, and Michèle had
been allotted the job of discreetly keeping an eye on the cooking, to make
sure that everything was washed and boiled. However, after a few meals it
became clear that the Sherpas were absolutely scrupulous about all hygienic
matters connected with us, although they themselves drank water of every
description without treating it and without giving it a second thought. Apparently they had learned that a trekker is a delicate creature who must be
treated with extreme care if he is to be kept moving.

As soon as the water came to a boil, tea was served—really a light meal
consisting of biscuits, sardines, cheese, peanut butter and jam, and sometimes Sherpa bread, a rich concoction made of millet and nuts. We were
then free to do what we liked until dinner, which was served between five-
thirty and six. During the interval, we washed, mended clothes and read,
and sometimes Jaccoux conducted a little clinic for any of the porters or
Sherpas who were ailing—mainly from sore throats and from infected blis-
ters acquired from walking barefoot, both of which responded very rapidly
to antibiotics. We also had a chance to study the scenery. What we saw the
first afternoon was typical of the Himalayan foothills in early fall. Everywhere we looked, there were rich fields of green set in terraces that climbed
the hills. The earth was carpeted with flowers in explosive tropical colors.
Sometimes we could make out a neat-looking village of stone houses, often
painted white and pink, some with wooden roofs and some with thatch
and some with slate. The Nepalese in the countryside have a keen sense of
color and are fond of brightly decorative flower gardens. If our campsite
afforded a view to the north, we could see the great Himalayan range—a
sort of distant white wall, with the summits so high that we often confused

them with clouds. Jaccoux wrote in his diary the first night, *"Sentiment de paradis."*

Dinner was always our gala meal. If it was warm enough, as it was on the first nights of our trek, we would eat outside, instead of in our tents, in the light of a candle or a kerosene lamp. (In the tropics the sun appears to set all at once, and by five-thirty or six it was night.) The first course was inevitably soup—usually powdered, but sometimes fresh chicken soup made from the remains of one of the birds the Sherpas had cooked. As we wandered through the villages, Ila would call out in Nepali to any of the local women who might have some fresh food to sell, *"Hay didi! Macha? Kukra? Phool? Phal?"*—"Hello, lady! Fish? Chicken? Eggs? Fruit?"—and sometimes he would be successful. If not, we ate rice and peas mixed with onions, and sometimes canned sausages and spaghetti. Later, when we got into the Sherpa country, we were treated to some of the Sherpa specialties like *mo-mo*—a delicious spiced dough wrapped around chopped mutton or goat and then fried crisp. Dessert was fruit—fresh tropical bananas, mangoes or mandarins, if they were available, or, if not, canned fruit from India. It was a thoroughly nourishing and adequate diet, but as the weeks wore on we began getting odd cravings for different tastes—Jaccoux had visions of *boudin* (baked blood pudding with apples), Michèle of red wine, and I of ice cream. We never managed to consume enough sugar to restore the energy that we expended walking ten or so miles a day—up and down—and when we returned to *chez* Boris in Kathmandu, thin as rakes, we fell like vultures on every rich dessert we could lay our hands on. By the end of the dinner, the Sherpas had put candles in our tents, and I was generally so tired that it was no trouble to fall asleep at seven or seven-thirty, while the Jaccoux read or played endless games of cards.

At our first camp, Ila suggested an early start the next day to escape the sun, so we agreed to get up at six-thirty and to drink a light tea in order to skip breakfast and get under way as quickly as possible. As the days went on, our rising time grew earlier and earlier; in our eagerness to avoid the heat we were usually on the trail well before six. Our second day was eventful in that, on the one hand, Jaccoux was bitten by a leech and, on the other, a new and remarkable Sherpa personality was revealed to us. The leech bite was completely unexpected. We had been bathing in a warm, azure jungle stream and had left our shoes on the bank. When Jaccoux started to put his shoes back on, he noticed that blood was flowing from between his toes. He removed a grisly-looking black leech by touching it with a cigarette ember—the classic method—applied alcohol and put his shoes on. Neither Michèle nor I was bitten, but it was a signal to watch out. As for the Sherpa, his name was Ang Dorje, and he was Ila's assistant. He had the broad, sad, wise face of a circus clown, and as I got to know him better I realized that he was one of the kindest people I had ever met. On the first day, my weakened ankle had been giving me a good deal of trouble, and I had used my parasol as a kind of crutch, which had not done much good. The following morning, when Ang Dorje appeared at my tent with tea, he was carrying a long stick that he had carved more or less in the form of a ski pole. "Horse," he said, giving it to me. From that day on, Ang Dorje and I and the "horse" were inseparable. Nothing was ever said, but whenever I was limping along the trail behind the rest of the group, I would notice Ang Dorje sitting on a rock a little way ahead of me and staring off into space, as if taking a rest. His resting places would always be at a point where the trail forked or where it was rough or slippery, and as I reached them he would materialize at my side discreetly, as if he just happened to be there by accident. It was never very clear to me how much English he understood. We carried on long conversations in which he taught me Sherpa words in exchange for their English equivalents, and I was confident that he followed everything I said. However, one very cold night we were camped in a small windy wooden cabin not far from Everest. Sherpas do not have chimneys in their houses; they leave the doors open to let out the smoke. This cabin did have a chimney, but the Sherpa domestic habits prevailed. I gave Ang Dorje a long and feeling discourse on how comfortable it would be in our cabin if the door were kept closed and the heat kept in, and he nodded sagely. Then he left the cabin, only to return a few minutes later, leaving the door open, and ask, as he pointed to it, "What English word this?" Curiously, if Ang Dorje had been a bit younger he would not have had to ask, for today the Nepalese educational system starts instruction in English at a very early age—as I later discovered to my advantage. One day, I was moving along the trail alone; the Jaccoux had raced off ahead, Ang Dorje had gone off for something, and the porters were far behind. Without paying much attention to where I was going, I found myself in a scrub jungle where the trail, as far as I could make out, completely disappeared. After wandering around aimlessly for half an hour or so, I began to get really worried that I was lost. To add to the general tone of things, the sun was setting, and I had just been bitten by a leech. At this point, a small Nepalese boy appeared from nowhere. He was carrying a large kukri and looked to be about ten. I began to gesticulate in the general direction of Tibet and to babble, "Sherpas, sahibs? Sherpas, sahibs?" in some desperation. He looked at me calmly and, in splendidly articulated English, said, "Where are you going?" Considerably abashed, I allowed myself to be led off in the direction of our party.

The days rolled on in a succession of jungle valleys, mountains, ridges, and rivers, and as we approached the high mountains the valleys grew steeper, the ridges higher, and rivers swifter and colder. Each morning, Ang Dorje would arrive at my tent with tea and an outline of the day's activities—"Some down-go river, river, birkpass, up-go steep road." (Breakfast was the other substantial meal of the day, with eggs, pancakes, toast, and coffee, and it was meant to do us from ten in the morning until teatime.) When we camped in towns, the children would come and surround our tent and stare at us and, at times, a man or a woman would come to us and ask for medicine for a child (if there is one English word that the Nepalese in the countryside know, it is "medicine"), and Jaccoux would try to find something in our pharmacy that would do some good. Once he told a mother whose baby was suffering with infected sores to wash the child with soap. She said that she did not have the money to buy soap, which cost one rupee (fourteen cents) and probably represented a day's wages. We gave her several bars of our soap.

The Swiss route that Roberts suggests is, in general, so arranged that all the camps are on high ground, which is dry and hence relatively free of jungle fauna. Sometimes, though, we found it convenient to do a stage and a half, especially if the following day featured an especially severe climb. (We would make the descent in the late afternoon so as to be able to climb in the very early cool morning.) Hence one night we camped in a tropical jungle near a stream. That night Ila displayed his talents as a barber. Michèle had been talking with Ila about his activities during the monsoon season and had learned about the barbering. Jaccoux is celebrated in Chamonix for his long, elegant blond plumage, and it was out of the question that he would submit to have any of it removed by a barber of unverified skills. On the other hand, I had forgotten to get a haircut before leaving France and my hair was beginning to curl down over my neck—an annoyance in the heat. So I became a willing victim. I was seated on a rubber poncho, and Ila went to work with a pair of scissors under the watchful gaze of our entire expeditionary force. Amid murmurs of general approval Ila proceeded to remove most of my mop, leaving a sort of crew cut. When it was over, Michèle commented, "*Ça te va,*" and that was that.

We decided to celebrate the event with a small toast with our expeditionary cognac, purchased in the New Delhi airport. One of the two bottles was brought out and we settled back to contemplate the tropical night. Suddenly something came hurtling out of the jungle, ran past our tents and jumped out at me. I leaped up in the air and emitted a bloodcurdling yelp, which brought Sherpas running from all directions. Ila, who had seen our visitor disappear into the jungle, said, "Eats snakes," from which I concluded it must have been a mongoose. It dawned on me that if it was a mongoose, it might well have been in search of its dinner. Jaccoux, armed with a long stick, led a thorough search of the tents but failed to turn up anything.

The next morning, as we walked through the jungle, we saw huge silver-gray gibbon-like monkeys swinging from tree to tree. Michèle and I were bitten by a leech, and after my bite we made a major scientific discovery. The leech had been removed by applying a cigarette to it—the Sherpas favor salt—and was lying in the grass still moving. It occurred to me that we might try an experiment on it. We had, more or less intact, our twelve cans of insect repellent, which had turned out, if anything, to attract the Himalayan flies, and which I had suggested we chuck into the nearest ravine since the cans were taking up space. Before doing this, we decided to spray the leech with the insect repellent to see what would happen. Instantly it curled up into a ball and died. We now had a first-rate antileech weapon, and during the next several days, until we reached the high mountain country, one of us always walked with the aerosol can of insect repellent at the ready.

After a week, we reached the important Hindu village of Those, which has a large school and an ancient ironworks, one of the few in Nepal. The village is located just on the frontier of Sherpa country; in fact, after leaving it we crossed an abrupt nine-thousand-foot pass, and, as if by magic, the character of the countryside, the people and the architecture was transformed. Since the Chinese invasion of Tibet there has been a sharp change in the attitude of the Sherpas toward Nepal. Until the invasion, they did not really regard themselves as Nepalese. ("Nepalese," to them, referred to the inhabitants of the Kathmandu Valley.) However, when the Chinese smashed the monasteries in Tibet and broke down the whole traditional structure of Tibetan society, the Sherpas began to turn toward their own government. In most Sherpa homes one sees, side by side, portraits of the Dalai Lama and the King of Nepal. The older generation of Sherpas have a deep-seated fear of the Chinese after what happened in Tibet; indeed, when I once visited an old lama in a small monastery south of Namche, he insisted on lifting up my sunglasses and looking at my eyes to be sure that I was not Chinese, before he would talk to me.

The Himalayan ridges have divided Nepal into small sections, and the ruggedness of the terrain keeps the different populations almost intact. We were now in Buddhist territory. The people had a definite Mongolian look, and the countryside was dotted with *chorten*—monuments in the shape of the contemplating Buddha. There were also numerous *mani* mounds (*mani* means "prayer" in Tibetan), usually erected in the middle of the trail and covered with carved stones on which the sacred formula "*Om mani padme hum*" was etched again and again. Sherpas passing a *mani* always leave it on their right, so that if they come back by the same trail they will have made a full circle around it, in deference to the full circle of the wheel of life. On each ridge, now sprinkled with snow, there would be a cluster of prayer flags printed with religious writings. The stone houses in the villages had small windows with wooden shutters that could be closed against the winter winds. (Glass is almost unknown in the Nepalese countryside.) We had definitely left the tropical jungles and the rice fields of the Himalayan foothills, and the cold nights told us that we were approaching the high mountains. We crossed a pass nearly twelve thousand feet high and felt the first effects of the thin air, which made us a little dizzy and short of breath. Coming down through some lovely pine forests, we reached the village of Junbesi—one of the largest and most attractive villages in the district of Solu. We had now been walking ten days, and although we had seen a number of high mountains, Everest had remained hidden behind the nearby hills. Ila promised us that if the sky was clear we might catch a glimpse of the mountain from a high ridge beyond Junbesi. The next morning, we churned up the ridge and from it got a stunning view of the Himalayan wall near Everest, but the Goddess Mother herself lay hidden in clouds. Ang Dorje flapped his arms and blew in a gallant attempt to disperse them, but after a half hour or so we gave up and continued along the trail to a campsite above the Dudh Kosi, the river that drains the whole south side of the Everest range.

We intended to follow the Dudh Kosi Valley up into the mountains, but first we had to cross the river and go through some low, damp fields. It had rained the night before—a last trace of the monsoon—and the trail was muddy, slippery and alive with leeches. I have never seen anything like it. Leeches were everywhere—on our shoes, our legs, our arms. I was bitten four times in ten minutes, and the legs of a porter in front of me were streaming with blood. We kept spraying ourselves with insect repellent, but every time we stopped to do this, more leeches attacked us. Finally Ila said, "Now quickly go!," and, all but running, we raced to higher ground. When we stopped, we were all thoroughly shaken. It was at this point that we began to wonder if it would be possible to come back by air. As it happened, every morning at about eight or so, when the sun began to beat down and we were starting up a hill, we had been hearing the sound of a small plane passing overhead. "Swiss people," Ila had said. "Lukla going." Lukla (alt. 9,200 feet) is a small village above the Dudh Kosi Valley; a few years ago, Edmund Hillary had carved a small grass airstrip out of a field on a hillside there. There are no regular flights to Lukla, but from time to time Mountain Travel, Roberts' outfit, is able to charter one or another of the STOL planes that are usually based in Kathmandu. It had been our original idea to walk to Namche and then fly out from Lukla, but this plan had been abandoned when it appeared that it would be difficult, if not impossible, to arrange a charter. Given the leeches, however, we thought we might take another crack at it. (As it turned out, the monsoon was over for good in a few days, and people who took our route a week or so later told us that it was completely dry, with not a leech in sight.)

Our hopes were raised a few hours later. I found the Jaccoux talking, in French, to a Sherpa on the trail. The Sherpa explained that he had learned French in Montpellier, where he had gone to study viticulture with the intention of growing grapes and making wine in the Kathmandu Valley. He had flown into Lukla in the morning to spend the Dassain holiday with his parents, who lived in the region, and his plane, he said, had returned to Kathmandu empty. A bit later, as we pushed along a wooden trail leading up the Dudh Kosi, we met a British Gurkha officer who had been in Namche on a holiday to see Everest, and he told us that behind him on the trail was a party of four—an Australian forester working in Nepal in the forest-conservation program, and three British ladies whom he was escorting. They had booked a plane out of Lukla in a day or so, the Gurkha told us, and could speak to the pilot to see if something might be arranged for us. After a few hours, we ran into the Australian and the three ladies, all looking fit and sunburned, and the forester said that he would be glad to talk to the pilot, and that we could expect to get a radio message at Dr. McKinnon's in a day or so. From reading Roberts' notes, I knew that there was a New Zealand doctor named John McKinnon who ran a small hospital—also set up by Hillary—in the Sherpa village of Khumjung, in the hills beyond Namche. The notes also mentioned a radio at the hospital, and our whole aviation scheme seemed to be falling into line. Little did we know.

That night we camped by a pair of excellent wooden bridges built in 1964—again by Hillary—across the Dudh Kosi and its adjoining tributary, the Bhote Kosi. The bridges have made an enormous contribution to the life of the Sherpas, since Namche is the trading center for the whole area and can now be reached from the lowlands by a relatively convenient trail; previously, crossing the rivers had been a major, risky operation. Our camp was on the Dudh Kosi itself, and from it no mountains could be seen at all, since they were blocked by the huge cliffs etched out by the river. However, the next day, given clear skies, we were promised a full and dramatic view of Everest and its satellites. By now, the winter weather pattern was beginning to settle in, which meant bright clear skies in the morning, followed by a clouding over in the afternoon and sometimes snow in the evening. To be as sure as possible of getting a good view, we left at the crack of dawn the next day. We were now over ten thousand feet— the lowest altitude we would be at for the next three weeks, but still sufficiently high so that we could not move too fast on the stiff uphill trudge toward Namche. As we climbed slowly, mountains began revealing themselves in all directions, and soon we were surrounded by great snow-covered peaks. Every now and again we would stop while Jaccoux took out his map and compass and tried to identify some of the mountains, to make sure we were not overlooking Everest. Up ahead, we saw a level place in the steep trail and an array of prayer flags near a *mani*—a sure sign that there was a special view of the snows. When we reached the *mani*, we looked to the north, up the valley, and fell into a stunned silence. First, like the brim of a glistening crown, we saw the massive ice wall of the Nuptse, perhaps ten miles away. Soaring above it was a black majestic pyramid, seamed with snow; from its top a plume of white floated off into space. It was Everest, and it looked like the Queen of the World. We stood fixed to the spot for nearly an hour, with all the Sherpas and Tibetans seated around us. Finally Ang Dorje said, "Beautiful. Now Namche go," and we started up the trail, which swung off to the left, hiding the mountains.

Ila had gone on ahead the night before to spend the evening with his family in Namche, and before we reached the village we were met by a lively-looking young boy who Ang Dorje said was Ila's son. Soon after, Namche appeared from around a bend. It is set in a horseshoe-shaped arena and clings to the side of an enormous gorge that drops down into the Bhote Kosi. There are about eighty stone houses in the village, and also a police checkpoint.* Our trail led right into the police station, where Ila was waiting, along with a couple of sleepy-looking Nepalese constables dressed in khaki. We had to hand over our trekking permits, and there was a lengthy pause while they were passed around, commented on and noted in various books. Next, we were taken to visit the district governor of Khumbu, a distinguished-looking former Nepalese Army officer named Colonel Bista. The Colonel greeted us in his pajamas and bathrobe and invited us to have morning tea with him while we explained where we had come from and where we planned to go. "If there is something I can do for you, let me know," he added—an offer that we were soon grateful for. In the meanwhile, Ila had set up our tents on a hillside a little above the town, and as it was clouding over and beginning to snow, we retired inside them.

During the afternoon, an almost endless series of Tibetans stopped by to sell us scrolls, rings, beads, bracelets, silver cups, and prayer wheels. We had just seen off the last vendor and had broken out what was left of the now remaining bottle of cognac we had brought along when a figure appeared outside our tent in the now driving snow. I peered out and saw a rather elegant-looking young man wearing white pajamalike pants, a somewhat oversized army overcoat and brightly colored wool gloves. Before I had a chance to say anything, he invited himself into the tent and introduced himself as Sub-Inspector Rana, of the Nepalese police. The name rang a bell. A

* There is also an Indian government wireless station, one of several near the Tibetan border, designed presumably to warn against any increase in Chinese border activity. Recently the Nepalese have asked the Indian government to remove them, and the Indians have threatened to fortify their now open frontier with Nepal.

few days before, we had met on the trail a young Swiss who had come to Namche without a trekking permit and had spent the better part of two weeks trying to arrange for one by telegraph. During this period, he passed a good deal of time discussing life and literature with Sub-Inspector Rana, whom he had come to regard as something of a cultural oasis and *bon vivant*. "Rana has a garden in which he grows six kinds of vegetables," the Swiss had told us.

We offered Rana a seat on one of the sleeping bags and a beaker of cognac.

"*Merzi, madame*," he said to Michèle, whose nationality he had apparently learned from studying our entry in the official book. "Do you pronounce it '*merzi*'?" he asked, and Michèle spent five minutes repeating "*merci*" over and over, until Rana's pronunciation was about right.

"You are an American," he said to me, and added, "I admire your John Steinbeck and your Agatha Christie," helping himself to another bit of brandy. In this general vein, the conversation flowed along until dinnertime, when we invited Rana to share our meal—which consisted mainly of rice, peas and onions. "I admire your onions, madame," he informed Michèle, who was staring gloomily at the now empty cognac bottle. We had told Rana that we planned to go to see Dr. McKinnon the next day, and he offered to join us, provided that the police station was in "perfect order" in the morning.

The next morning there was no Rana, so, assuming that the police station had not been in the best order, we left for Khumjung and the McKinnons. Khumjung is a typical high Sherpa village. It is at 12,300 feet and consists of a large number of sturdy-looking stone houses set among yak pens and potato fields. The walk from Namche to Khumjung is surely one of the most beautiful in the world. On it one sees another group of the satellites of Everest, especially Ama Dablam. While Everest impresses one with its size, Ama Dablam, which is only 22,595 feet, impresses one with its elegance. It is a perfectly shaped mountain—a sort of ice Matterhorn—with steep faces of delicately fluted ice. (It was first climbed in 1961 by a mixed New Zealand–American group. The sole American in the party, Barry Bishop, who later climbed Everest, was in Nepal when we were there, and he said that Ama Dablam was technically more difficult than Everest by several orders of magnitude, although much lower.)

Leaving the fields and the yak pens, we followed a series of neat paths up to a modern building—the Khumjung hospital. The McKinnons, both in their twenties, turned out to be an extremely cordial and attractive couple. He said that he had first come to Nepal with Hillary in 1964 when he was still a student, to climb and to help build the bridges. He fell in love with the country, and two years later, when Hillary succeeded in building a hospital with funds raised through his speaking tours in New Zealand and with private contributions, McKinnon volunteered to be its first doctor, a post he held until 1968 when he returned to New Zealand. It would be difficult to imagine a better choice. He and his wife, Diane, who taught English in one of the Hillary schools (since 1961, Hillary, with the aid of the local villagers, has built six schools in the Solu-Khumbu area, which will eventually be absorbed into the expanding Nepalese public-education system), succeeded in immersing themselves in the life of the community. (Sometime later, Mrs. McKinnon took us to visit one of the Sherpa schools. It was a two-room affair in a modern quonset-hut-like structure. The "headmaster" was a multilingual Sherpa from Darjeeling. Although it was November, the school was about to close for a long winter recess, since many of the pupils were to leave for the lowlands with their parents, who had homes in the lower valleys where the winters are less severe. The major school term is in the spring and summer. The children, perhaps a hundred of them of various ages, were engaged in their English lessons and were reciting in loud choruses. I noticed several English mottoes on the walls, including "God Bless Our King" and "Fortune Has Wings," and wondered if any of the children realized how much "wings" in the form of the airplane had to do with their futures. The increasingly active link that the Sherpas have with the rest of Nepal is coming to depend more and more on the fact that Solu-Khumbu can now be reached fairly conveniently by air. Perhaps Namche Bazar or Khumjung will one day be transformed into the Chamonix or Zermatt of Asia, with a profusion of hotels all guaranteeing fine views of Everest. It is both a heartening and a somewhat dreary prospect.)

Being a doctor in Solu-Khumbu is not a passive matter, since the Sherpas have had relatively little experience with modern medicine and until recently were inclined to put their faith in spirit mediums and magic potions. McKinnon had to prove that modern medicine is more effective than looking into the silver mirror of a spirit medium, and to do so he had to put in many miles of walking over very steep terrain to visit his patients, since Sherpas who feel that they are really sick prefer to stay in their own houses and die. Treatment is free. The most persistent problems are tuberculosis and goiter. Goiter, which is brought on by a lack of iodine in the diet, is common throughout the Himalayas, because such iodine as there is in the soil is removed by erosion and not replaced by the rains, which are iodine-free, the mountains being so far from the sea. There is now a move to make the import of iodized salt obligatory (Nepal has no salt of its own), and this may well solve the goiter problem. But in the meantime whole villages in Solu-Khumbu are afflicted with the disease and, what is worse, there is a high incidence of cretinism among the children. Until the diet could be changed, McKinnon attempted to treat his people with iodine tablets and iodized oil. There is a problem of knowing just how big a dose to administer, and he conducted a series of experiments to find out. I nearly gave him a fit when I innocently announced that we had been dispensing iodine on our walk. What I meant was that we had been treating cuts with liquid iodine, but he assumed that we had been handing out tablets. A few years ago, some well-meaning trekkers came through and did hand out iodine tablets indiscriminately, which threw McKinnon's work off for months.

Tuberculosis is a much more serious matter. It is hard to detect in the early stages, unless a Sherpa is willing to come in to Khumjung for an X ray or, at least, a skin test. Moreover, the treatment, while very effective, is lengthy. No Sherpa can afford to spend a year or so in a hospital. McKinnon worked out a program that allows Sherpas with tuberculosis to live in a wing of the hospital for three months—with their families, if necessary—and then return to their villages. In each village he trained two people to act as nurses. They can give the necessary shots twice a week, and they know enough about the symptoms to recognize if someone appears to need help. In Namche I met one of McKinnon's "nurses," who turned out to be a very intelligent fifteen-year-old boy. He was, among other things, responsible for treating Ila's wife. In addition, McKinnon gave all the children in the area skin tests and smallpox vaccinations. Even as late as 1963, when the American Everest expedition came through Solu-Khumbu, whole villages were being ravaged by smallpox epidemics. It was about that time that Hillary started his vaccination program which saved many lives and which was carried on by McKinnon.

During the monsoon, the McKinnons hardly ever saw any Europeans, and such rare mail as they got was carried to the hospital by porters. In the winter, many of the Sherpas head south. They are quite nomadic, and it is common for a family to have as many as three houses—one in the high mountain country, one in a village like Khumjung, and a third down below, where it is relatively warm in the winter. McKinnon says that he did not miss either his mail or his visitors, since he and his wife shared the social life of the Sherpas—the weddings, the naming ceremonies (a baby is named by its grandparents in a lively ceremony in which a good deal of *chang*, the local beer made of corn or rice, is drunk), and the funerals (Sherpas cremate their dead, as do the Hindus of southern Nepal. The Hindus preserve part of a bone from the cremation and bury it in one of the sacred rivers beside which cremations take place.) He was also engaged in a potato experiment. The potato is the cornerstone of the Sherpa diet, although, oddly enough, it seems to be a relatively new arrival in Solu-Khumbu. Christoph von Fürer-Haimendorf, a noted anthropologist who has made an extensive study of the Sherpas, noted, in his book *The Sherpas of Nepal*, that "it is certain that the potato was not known in the Himalayas until comparatively recently and the two most likely sources of its spread into Eastern Nepal are the gardens of European settlers in Darjeeling and the garden of the British residency in Kathmandu." This would make the potato less than a hundred years old in Solu-Khumbu, and Fürer-Haimendorf connects this dating to the time when the monasteries were built in Solu-Khumbu. There have been monasteries in Tibet for centuries, but the monasteries in Solu-Khumbu are quite new. The thought is that they were built and monks were allowed to withdraw from the population after the introduction of the potato gave the Sherpas enough food so that not everyone was required to scratch crops from the rather meager soil. The Sherpa "method" of growing potatoes is to throw the plants into the ground and to hope for the best. McKinnon took a plot of land belonging to the hospital and cultivated half of it Sherpa style and half of it using careful agricultural methods. What he found, perhaps not surprisingly, was that on the careful half he grew twice as many potatoes as on the Sherpa half and that the potatoes were larger and freer of blight. He hoped the lesson was beginning to sink in.

Among the letters that McKinnon had received in the last delivery from Lukla before our arrival was one from Mountain Travel saying that space was available for a flight to Kathmandu on the second of November—in about two and a half weeks—for three people. However, we learned to our dismay that McKinnon had no radio—one had been ordered but had not arrived—so we had no way of communicating with Kathmandu. McKinnon said that our only chance was to persuade the authorities in Namche to send a wire to Mountain Travel on the police wireless, and to pray that it got there. Leaving Khumjung, we walked back to Namche to look for Sub-Inspector Rana in the hope that we could convince him to send the wire. We stopped by the police station, which was manned by a lone constable who, from time to time, jumped from his desk to chase an errant goat out of Rana's vegetable garden.

In due time, Rana was found. *"Bon soir, madame,"* he said to Michèle, bowing, kissing her hand, and apologizing for not appearing in the morning. We explained our plight, and after thinking the matter over he said, "I would, of course, like to help you. But it would be very courteous if first you were to talk to Colonel Bista. If he signs the telegram, then I would be honored to send it by our very wireless."

Colonel Bista was engaged in the nightly volleyball game that took place between the police and the soldiers in Namche, and we had to wait a half hour or so before we could see him. I had, in the meanwhile, written out a telegram, which the Colonel, when he was free, read very carefully, offering a few suggestions for its amplification, and then signed, remarking that it was the Dassain holiday in Kathmandu and he was not sure how soon it would be delivered. In any case, we had done what we could, and the next day we were off to the base of Everest with the understanding that if an answer ever came through it would be sent up by runner.

The following morning, our Tibetan porters showed up early. They were dressed in heavy clothes, and instead of the Chinese-made basketball shoes that they had been wearing since leaving Kathmandu, they now wore wonderfully colorful heavy cloth boots with thick soles. Ila appeared with some expedition gear, including a down-filled sleeping bag, that he had used with the Indian expedition at an altitude of 26,000 feet on Everest. "Next days, some cold," he announced. The evenings had already been "some cold," and we were putting on more and more clothes to keep from freezing. However, the day of our departure was bright and warm, and we set out for the Thyangboche monastery, the home of the reincarnated lama who is the religious leader of the Sherpas of Solu-Khumbu. It was a beautiful walk, with Everest and all of her satellites in full view, and in a few hours we struggled up a steep hill, 12,600 feet high, where the monastery was and into a nearby cabin built by an Indian expedition for Everest trekkers. It is drafty, but Hillary—leave it to Hillary—built a splendid woodburning stove in the living room which keeps everything warm as long as one continues to feed it and keeps the doors shut. The walls are covered with signatures of members of former Everest expeditions and trekkers who have spent the night there. For us, it was the first time in more than two weeks that we had slept in a building, and we were happy over the change. Ila had promised us a visit to the head lama before we headed off into the mountains, and for that purpose he had bought three white ceremonial scarves, which we were meant to present to the lama; in return, he would give each of us one of his own scarves.

The head lama of Thyangboche was chosen for his role while still a small child. He comes from a Sherpa family in Namche, and when he was very young he began to talk about his "home" in Thyangboche, where he had never been. The monks at Thyangboche, hearing of this, got some of the clothes of their head lama, who had just died, and mixed them with objects not belonging to the lama. The child, who was then four, picked out the clothes of the old monk and said that they belonged to him. He was immediately heralded as the reincarnation of the old lama and brought to Thyangboche to study. When he was sixteen, he was sent to Tibet for more study, and in 1956 he came back to Thyangboche as its abbot. He is now in his early thirties. I was immensely impressed by him. He speaks no English, but his brother does, and he acted as our interpreter when Ila's English failed. The abbot's apartment is simple, but he has many modern devices— a radio, a camera, a watch—that have been given to him over the years by people on expeditions. Apart from study, religious ceremonies and running the affairs of the monastery—the monks depend partly on donations and partly on a certain amount of commerce that they carry on in the community and in Tibet—the abbot's main interest is in flowers. He has a small hothouse, which he and his brother built to protect his flowers during the winter. Friends send him seeds from all over the world, and he has a book filled with all the seed envelopes, along with the names of the donors. The abbot accepted our scarves and took three of his own and touched them to his forehead as a blessing. While this was happening, Ila stood beaming. It was obviously a ceremony that meant a great deal to him, and he later told me that he would not go into the high mountains without the blessing of the abbot.

One of the things that I discussed with the abbot was the yeti—the legendary Abominable Snowman. It is safe to say that no reliable Western observer has ever seen one, although some curious bearlike tracks have been photographed on the remote glaciers near Everest. On the other hand, the yeti does play a persistent role in the mythology of the region. Sometimes it is given semihuman characteristics, sometimes it is said to carry people off, but most often it is said to look like a bear or, perhaps, some sort of simian. The abbot had never seen one, either, but he said that when the snows are very heavy around the monastery some of the other abbots claim to have seen such a creature. (Among the Sherpas it is usually a distant cousin or an uncle, now passed on, who saw one once.) He told us that in one of the monasteries down the valley there were a scalp and a hand (a bone from a hand) that were claimed by the local authorities there to be from a yeti. At this point the abbot smiled and pointed to a chair which was obviously covered by a goatskin and said, through his brother, "It is the same kind of yeti as this." Later we visited the monastery itself, and for a small donation the ancient abbot there produced the objects in question. Ang Dorje, who, I gathered, did not have a very high opinion of the yeti question in general, donned what is presumably a goat scalp, and we took his picture with great solemnity. Most of the other Sherpas seemed to take the whole thing as a joke, so we did not learn anything more about the yeti than we knew before we went to Nepal.

We left Thyangboche and headed north. The villages became cruder and cruder, and the terrain more barren. The tree line in the Himalayas is very high, and we were now at nearly fourteen thousand feet—the altitude of a good-sized Swiss Alp—and it was still grazing land for yaks. Wood was scarce, so we used dried yak dung for fuel. It makes an excellent smokeless, odorless fire. On the trail we passed yak caravans being driven down for the winter. The yak is a great, shaggy beast, but incredibly timid; it will all but climb a vertical bank to get out of one's way on the trail. (I did once encounter an aggressive yak. Not far from Thyangboche, I was walking along peacefully when I heard several people ahead croaking "Ee-yuk, Eee-yuk"—a series of sounds that the Sherpas make if there are yaks around.

Above the general din I heard Michèle yelling, *"Attention,* Jeremy—*un yak fou!"* I looked up and found myself staring into the eyes of a rather malicious-looking brown yak that was attached by a string to a Sherpa who was trying to restrain it. It lowered its horns, and I went up a rock embankment in very great haste, and stayed there until the animal was led away.) The Sherpas have great affection for yaks. (One night, we heard some piercing cries not far from our camp, and I at once thought of a leopard, since I had read in a book on the British Everest expedition that its camp had been visited by one after dark. Moreover, Jaccoux claimed that he could make out a pair of glittering eyes off in the scrub. But when I asked a Sherpa what kind of animal it was, he replied, "Doesn't eat yaks," which seemed to settle the matter. It was probably a small wildcat of some kind.) Being Buddhist, the Sherpas will not, in general, kill any animal, but if a yak should happen to drop dead, or if someone else should kill it, they are delighted to eat the meat. Sherpas are profoundly religious, but not dogmatic. As Buddhists, their greatest concern is to add to their *sönam.* There are many ways that one can increase one's *sönam.* For example, a rich man can increase it by having a temple built for the community. There are some very wealthy Sherpas in Solu-Khumbu. Namche Bazar was the great trading station on the way to Tibet, and before 1950 enormous yak trains passed through the town en route to the Nangpa La, a nineteen-thousand-foot pass leading to Tibet. From Tibet, Sherpas got salt, copperware (all the cooking utensils in Solu-Khumbu are of copper—and very beautiful, too—although now they are being supplanted by tin and aluminum objects, usually of Chinese manufacture), and animals, for which they traded rice, carried up from the lowlands, and dyes, among other things. Even now there is some trading into Tibet, and it is a very profitable business. We were told of one trader who came back from Tibet with a profit of eighty thousand Nepalese rupees —about $8,000—from the sale of one yak train's worth of goods. He was building a small temple in Namche, and while we were there we watched the famous Sherpa artist Kapa Kalden in the process of decorating the interior and the huge prayer wheel. One can also lose *sönam.* In his book on the Sherpas, Fürer-Haimendorf gives a list of some of the sins that can lead to loss of *sönam.* It is an extraordinary list, and it gives an idea of why people who have come to know the Sherpas are so fond of them. Among the items are the following:

1. To threaten children or make them cry is sin, whatever the reason.

2. To fell trees is sin, though on occasion it is inevitable; even to pluck flowers is sin, and it is sinful to set fire to the forest.

3. To marry a girl who is unwilling is sin both for the husband and for her parents, who arranged for the marriage.

4. To talk ill of someone behind his back is sin, particularly if what one tells about him is not true.

We camped in some deserted yak pens in Pheriche, a summer village, now abandoned, since the yaks had gone below for the winter. The nights were now desperately cold. As long as the sun was up, it was quite comfortable, but as soon as the shadows began to creep over the ground the temperature plummeted to near zero, and we made a dash for the tents, to put on every ounce of warm clothes we had brought along. It was much too cold to bathe, and Jaccoux said that it would be inadvisable even to wash, since the dry air was so dehydrating that we risked being severely burned and chapped by the sun. By now, we were all beginning to feel the effects of the altitude—headaches and dizziness. The streams that led down from the Khumbu Glacier—the glacier that comes down from the sides of Everest—were frozen, and we crossed them gingerly. Our next, and highest, camp was at sixteen thousand feet—higher than the summit of Mont Blanc —and the three of us were beginning to feel truly worn down by the altitude and the cold. We were merely a mile or two from the Tibetan border. This is the only place in Nepal where the government allows one to get that close to the border, since the way is blocked by the Everest range and it would take a full-scale alpine expedition to cross it; trekkers have all they can do to haul themselves up to the high yak pastures. However, we could see some of the peaks in Tibet, and also the Lo La and the Shangri La. "La" is the Tibetan word for "pass," and Shangri La is an impressive but bleak-looking pass that leads into Tibet.

We now began to find out for ourselves why the Sherpas and the Tibetans do so well on the high climbing expeditions. While we were literally trembling with cold and fatigue, Ang Dorje was wandering around happily in a light shirt and wearing tennis shoes with no socks. I asked Ila if the altitude ever bothered him, and he said, "Twenty-six thousand feet, some headache getting." At sixteen thousand feet my head felt like a melon. The next day, we climbed the Kala Pattar. By any standard, it is a *montagne à vache* —a gentle, grassy slope with a few rocks on top. But the summit is at 18,100 feet—2,300 feet higher than any mountain in Europe—and I found it very tough going. I seemed to be held back by a sort of invisible wall, and every time I moved I felt as if I were hauling a ton of bricks. From the summit we got an incredible view of Everest and the Khumbu Glacier. Everest was perhaps a mile away, but the summit was still two miles above us. I asked Jaccoux, who had been to 22,200 feet in Peru, how people could climb at such heights. (I was having all I could do to walk.) He said that of course they trained for weeks before the summit climb. In addition, there was a morale factor that comes from being part of a large, dedicated group; also when one actually comes to grips with the difficulties of the mountain, one tends to forget one's aches and pains. It was now beginning to snow, and we hurried down. In passing, we had a chance to look at the memorial tablet that the American expedition had erected to Jake Breitenbach, the climber who was killed on the Khumbu ice fall in 1963. (Just this year his remains were discovered on the Khumbu Glacier.) When we got back to our tents, it was snowing heavily. I was so tired that when Jaccoux handed me a headache pill I just stood there holding it, not knowing what to do with it. I somehow got back in my tent and lay gasping on my sleeping bag. After a few minutes, the head of Ang Dorje appeared in the tent. "Soup ready," he announced, and in came a tray of warm tomato soup and crackers. He stood there while I ate it, to make sure that I was all right, and then left.

We had had some vague plans to do more climbing and hiking, but the snow was coming down in thick gusts, and we were really exhausted by the altitude. So the next morning we began the trip back. On the first day, we passed a huge lake, ice blue, that nestled against the mountains. "In summer, many yaks," Ang Dorje told us. When we got a little farther down, we were met by a runner from McKinnon bearing a letter from Mountain Travel that had just arrived. The office had received both our telegram and a personal message from the Australian forester, and we could take the plane on the second of November.

We had several days to fill before that date, some of which we passed in the monastery grounds in Thyangboche, some with the McKinnons, and some in Namche. In Namche, Sub-Inspector Rana told us that while we were gone a yak had got into his garden with the six kinds of vegetables and had eaten every last one of them. Ang Dorje and Ila and a small group of our Tibetan porters had to hurry back to Kathmandu to meet some new trekkers, whom they were taking to western Nepal, near Annapurna. To make sure that we didn't get into any trouble and were fed periodically, Mountain Travel had assigned two young Sherpas to look after us until the plane came. They were eighteen, and at first I was worried about how two young boys would fare as cooks and guides. There was no need for concern. Both of them had been on expeditions since they were fourteen, both had gone to the Hillary schools, and they spoke excellent English. They were dressed in Western-style blue jeans, and when we left Namche for Lukla one of them was carrying a transistor radio on which he listened to music from Radio Nepal and India.

For the next three days, we camped next to the tiny airfield. The boys turned out to be fine cooks, and we feasted on pancakes and chapatties— Sherpa unleavened bread. Each morning at about sunrise, the Swiss plane came in to leave off people. It was not yet our turn to go, and the pilot informed us rather tersely that we would have to wait until it was. One morning the passengers turned out to be the German ambassador to Nepal and the United Nations High Commissioner for Refugees; they had come up to look at some Tibetan refugee villages. Another morning, a U.S. AID helicopter came floating in with a passenger who said that he had been sent by the Smithsonian Institution to collect Tibetan manuscripts. At eight-forty every morning we got the English-language news broadcast from Kathmandu. Otherwise we sat around, somewhat bored, waiting for our plane. Finally, on November 2nd, as scheduled, it came in over the mountains. We had been joined by two trekkers also waiting to be flown out, and the five of us piled into the plane with our gear. There was the inevitable Nepalese observer from the Foreign Office wedged into one of the back seats among the rucksacks. The plane took off, and for the next hour we saw unfolding beneath us the whole route that we had taken over the previous month. There were the tiny trails that we had climbed up and down, over steep ridges and through the terraced fields and jungles. Here and there we could spot a familiar village clinging to a mountainside, and to the north we could see the great white mountains, with the clouds hovering near their summits. As I looked at them, I thought of a Nepalese legend that tells how they came to Nepal. In the beginning, the mountains, which were the oldest children of the god Prajapati, all had wings, and they flew about the world as they liked. However, Indra, the god of rain, wished to bring the waters to the people of Nepal. So he cut the wings from the mountains, which then fell to earth and could no longer fly. The wings became clouds, and still cling to the mountains. So wherever there are mountains there are clouds, and water from their rain nourishes the earth beneath.

4

L'Envoi

$\mathcal{F}$osco Maraini, the noted Italian travel writer, in his book about Asian travel, *Where Four Worlds Meet*, introduces the notion of voyages of the first and second "type." In a voyage of the first type the traveler never really crosses a cultural frontier no matter how far he may actually have traveled. He may encounter new languages or religions or the people may appear very different, but in a subtle way these differences only emphasize the common elements that the voyager shares with the peoples he is visiting. As Maraini puts it, there is "some fundamental essence common to both your country and theirs. You are still within the orbit of those peoples who developed and matured together, to a greater or lesser degree, through thousands of years of history. . . . They will all tell their pupils *something* about Christ and Aristotle, Moses and Homer, Shakespeare, Dante, and Goethe, Descartes, Galileo, Beethoven, Cervantes and the rest, right down to Tolstoy and Van Gogh. But bring up such names as Jalal-ud-din Rumi or Valkami, Nagarjuna or Milarepa, Lao-tzu or Chu Hsi, Genghis Khan or Hideyoshi, and you realize that you are treading on ground which (at least as things are at present) is basically alien, exotic, to be cultivated only by specialists: something concerning other 'fields of intelligibility' than one's own. You have crossed the ideological barrier"—and thus have made a voyage of the second type.

Even in a country as "exotic," from our point of view, as Nepal, it is possible for a traveler to so limit his contacts that the "cultural frontier" is perceived dimly if at all—from, for example, the window of a rapidly moving automobile. As the country "develops"—moves more and more toward acquiring the technological standards of the West—it becomes easier for a visitor to ignore ideological barriers completely. This is, in a way, a pity, since one of the most fascinating things about Nepal is just this cultural frontier. In Nepal one may discover how a people—or, really, many separate peoples—evolving in all but total isolation from the West came to deal with the great realities that affect human beings: death, love, birth, law and the meaning of life itself. As we in the West face these realities, we bring with us a vast tradition of what we like to think of as rational inquiry. We have come to believe that there are "scientific" explanations of most things, and for most of us this is a source of comfort, since what we can explain in terms of scientific principles we can also, to some extent, manipulate. It is reassuring to know that microbes cause disease, for microbes can be destroyed. It is reassuring to know that lightning is an electrical discharge, for physics then teaches us how to act so as to minimize the risk of being felled by a lightning bolt. In truth, of course, most of us understand as much about the underlying scientific explanations of these natural phenomena as we do about the magical incantations of the spirit mediums of Nepal. But we are usually willing to accept this partial understanding, since the incantations of our scientists, even our computers, lead to effective and practical solutions to many of our problems.

For a Westerner to get a feeling for the cultural life of Nepal, and especially of rural Nepal, he must try to imagine living in an extremely vivid natural environment, frequently hostile, surrounded by mountains, jungles, wild animals, often plagues, without doctors to cure the sick, without electric lights to illuminate the night, and, above all, without our scientific tradition that informs us that what we see around us can be explained by natural laws and principles.* In such an environment every object of nature becomes charged with mystical powers. The Himalayan snows floating above the Nepalese countryside in serene, remote grandeur become the abodes of gods. The smooth stones of the rivers become charged with magical powers, and even the animals become representatives of unseen but powerful forces.

In 1954 Giuseppe Tucci, an Italian scholar and Orientalist, who has made eight journeys into Tibet and six in Nepal, took an extensive trip by foot in central Nepal. He was in search of the origins of the Malla kings, the dynasty that ruled the country, or at least parts of the country, from the fifteenth to the eighteenth century. (He found traces of the Mallas in some of the remote central hill towns and concluded that there was evidence that linked them to prior Indian nobility.) On his way back south toward the Indian frontier, Tucci came upon one of his Nepalese guides in a striking attitude of prayer alongside the trail. Tucci writes:

I saw the man who led the march and who was acting as our guide standing with his hands raised in prayer. At his feet was a cobra with distended hood watching him threateningly. But he did not move and would have preferred to be bitten rather than kill it. The snake is a naga, a mysterious creature linked with the obscure forces of the underworld, which guards the treas-

---

* The closest thing to a scientific tradition in Nepal is the practice of astrology. There is no doubt that astrology plays a very important role in the life of the Nepalese. For example, the date of the wedding of the Crown Prince, Birendra, to a Rana—February 27, 1970—was decided in collaboration with the Court astrologers. Very recently I was told of an incident involving a Nepalese village child that shows just how deep the faith in astrology runs in the countryside. When the child was born it had a bad horoscope, and, unhappily, six months later, the child's father died. The mother, because of its horoscope, blamed the death on the child and left it to starve. It was found in this condition by a U.S. AID worker and eventually was adopted, with a special dispensation from the King, by a U.S. AID official. The child, a young boy whom I met in Kathmandu, appears to be thriving, although his new father says that, according to the horoscope, his eighth year should be a difficult one. In his twenties, however, he is expected, if all goes well, to take a long and profitable voyage of some three years to a distant place.

ures hidden in the womb of the earth and the springs which give it life, it is the symbol of Shiva, the sign of time that always renews itself. Between killing and being killed many would still choose the second alternative.

As should be clear from the earlier parts of this book, an increasingly large number of Nepalese would find this kind of primitive religious expression as strange as we do. In an interview given to the *New York Times* reporter Joseph Lelyveld a few years ago, the King was asked if he himself believed that he was the reincarnation of the god Vishnu, a traditional Nepalese belief. King Mahendra replied, "Personally speaking, I don't believe in all those things. First of all I am a human being. And whatever I am, I must serve my country." However, the traces of the ancient religious attitudes are in Nepal, and the farther one travels into the remote countryside, the more they merge with present practice and belief.

The ambiguities in the religious attitudes of the Nepalese are nowhere more evident than in their art. There does not seem to be a tradition of secular art in Nepal, unless one wishes to count the Newar building decorations or the few rather stilted portraits of the early kings. Art in Nepal is an essentially religious activity. It has been remarked that Himalayan art differs from Indian or Chinese or even traditional Tibetan art, with which it has pronounced similarities, by a kind of savage dynamism. The Nepalese Buddhas are not always serene, and their expressions frequently appear to exhibit cruelly ironic smiles. Gods and their consorts merge with each other in a frenzy of sexual energy. (One of the more striking aspects of the temples of Kathmandu are the erotic carvings that often decorate friezes around the pillars supporting the pagoda roofs. These carvings, oddly stylized as if illustrating a text, have an almost comic-strip effect. One theory is that they were put there to offend the goddess of lightning, a prudish female, and so to encourage her to avoid the temple. Another theory is that they are a kind of manual for the performance of Tantric rites, communal sexual acts—still practiced, it is said, in parts of Nepal. One Nepalese commentator that I read speculated that the carvings had no special religious significance but were simply an expression of the joy and vigor of life. One of the chief characteristics of the carvings, though, is their very lack of joyousness and their strong sense of ritual.) Even the carvings and metal castings of animals, often half-human, have a savagery about them. It is as if the cruelties of the nature around the artists who created these works was being explained in terms of the cruelties of the unseen gods and goddesses.

It is not entirely clear what these religious symbols mean to contemporary Nepalese themselves. No week goes by in Nepal without some sort of religious festival. (One of the most remarkable is the Indra Jatra, an eight-day festival celebrated to propitiate the rain god Indra. On the third day a "living goddess," a young girl chosen in infancy by the priests of the Kumari Temple in Kathmandu, who then passes her life, until puberty, sequestered in a special apartment in the temple, is paraded through the streets of the city. Her only public appearances until the Indra Jatra are at a balcony window in the temple, where, dressed and made up almost like a costume doll, she will occasionally cast an aloof and languid eye on visitors assembled in the courtyard below. But during the Indra Jatra she is carried through the streets of Kathmandu in a chariot for all to see. After puberty she is free to marry—but it is thought that marrying her brings bad luck, even death, to the groom, so she is likely to spend her life a spinster.) Among the most beautiful Nepalese holidays is the Tihar, the festival of light, which occurs in the autumn, when the nights in Kathmandu are clear and quite warm. All of the houses are decorated with lights, usually oil lamps, and the entire city glows in a lovely flickering illumination. The first night of the five-day festival is dedicated to the crows, which are offered food to placate them, since the crow is regarded in Nepalese mythology as the messenger of death. These festivals are a fundamental part of Nepalese life, and the obviously profound feelings that are associated with them are clear to anyone who has witnessed them. On the other hand, the temples, which at night are places of worship, and where Nepalese go who have come to Kathmandu from the countryside for a festival or to sell their agricultural produce and have no other place to stay, sleep and eat, during the day become market bazaars. The bases of statues are covered with baskets full of fruits and merchandise—sandals, razor blades, shoelaces, kitchen utensils, herbs and tea. Just below a statue of Ganesh, the elephant god, one may well find a Nepalese barber plying his trade. In the temples and religious sanctuaries in the countryside, often all but abandoned, one comes upon totems, carvings of figures half demon and half animal, whose religious significance now seems lost even to the Nepalese. These works of art, often remarkably beautiful and usually in a state of physical decay, lie in some sort of limbo between religious icons and secular museum pieces.

Village life, with its endless swirl of animals, lively children and farming activities, appears to flow around them as if they were not there.

In the last analysis, all of the endlessly complex and varied religious traditions of Nepalese life demonstrate the infinite and often beautiful ways that human beings have evolved to adapt to the realities of the world. As I have tried to indicate, these realities are in transition in Nepal as the Nepalese, and especially the rural Nepalese, increasingly come into contact with modern science and technology. Many of these changes, perhaps most of them, are for the better. Yet a traveler to Nepal, charmed by the people and the country, sometimes finds himself wishing that change could come about without destroying too much of what is so lovely in Nepalese life, and without importing too much of what appears to be destroying the beauty of Western environments like our own. Perhaps this wish is impossible and, in making it, one is committing what has been called by Jacques Barzun "the fallacy of utopian addition"—the acceptance of technological progress without paying the price that goes with it. In any event, there are so many pressing, urgent problems in Nepal—problems that can be dealt with in terms of modern technology and that must be dealt with now if the country is to prosper—that it will be a long time before Nepal shares with us the problems of a civilization overburdened by its technology.

Selected Bibliography

Bista, Dor Bahadur, *People of Nepal*. Kathmandu: Government of Nepal, Department of Publicity, 1967.

Buhler, Jean, *Nepal*. Lausanne: Éditions Rencenive, 1964.

Chevalley, Gabriel, *et al.*, *Avant-Premières à l'Everest*. Paris: Arthaud, 1953.

Fürer-Haimendorf, Christoph von, *The Sherpas of Nepal*. Berkeley: University of California Press, 1964.

Hagen, Tony, *Nepal*. Berne: Kümmerly & Frey, 1961.

Harrer, Heinrich, *Seven Years in Tibet*. New York: E. P. Dutton & Co., 1954.

Hornbein, Thomas F., *Everest, The West Ridge*. San Francisco: Sierra Club, 1965.

Hunt, Sir John, *The Conquest of Everest*. New York: E. P. Dutton & Co., 1954.

Joshi, Bhuwan L., and Leo Rose, *Democratic Innovations in Nepal*. Los Angeles: University of California Press, 1966.

Landon, Percival, *Nepal*. London: Constable, 1928.

Lévi, Sylvain D., *Dans l'Inde*. Paris: F. Reider & Co., 1925.

Maraini, Fosco, *Where Four Worlds Meet*. New York: Harcourt, Brace & World, 1964.

Mihaly, Eugene Bramer, *Foreign Aid and Politics in Nepal*. London: Oxford University Press, 1965.

Morris, John, *A Winter in Nepal*. London: Hart-Davis, 1963.

———, *Nepal and the Gurkhas*. London: Her Majesty's Stationery Office, 1965.

Peissel, Michel, *Tiger for Breakfast*. New York: E. P. Dutton & Co., 1966.

———, *Mustang, The Forbidden Kingdom*. New York: E. P. Dutton & Co., 1967.

Regmi, D. R., *A Century of Family Autocracy in Nepal*. Banaras: Commercial Printing Works, 1950.

Snellgrove, David L., *Buddhist Himalaya*. Oxford: Cassirer, 1957.

Tucci, Giuseppe, *Nepal: In Search of the Malla*. New York: E. P. Dutton & Co., 1962.

Ullman, James Ramsey, *Man of Everest: Tenzing*. London: George Harrap & Co., 1956.

Index

[*Page numbers in italics indicate illustrations.*]

Abominable Snowman, the, 162
Adams, Barbara, 8
Aid programs in Nepal, foreign, 70, 73, 74, 75, 76, 80, 81–83, 87, 90–95
Aircraft based in Nepal, 55–58
Airfields in Nepal, 56–57, 58
Air travel to Nepal, international, 58–59

American Everest expedition (1963), 79, 133–34, 158
Amshuvarma, 22
Animal sacrifice, 23, 146
Annapurna Hotel, 67
Annapurna mountain range, 17, 58, 59, 69, 112, 135
Anthrax epidemics, 74

Arabs, 92
Art in Nepal, 174–75
Astrology, 173n.
Aufschnaiter, Peter, 91–92
Australia, 92
Avant-Premières à l'Everest, 140

Bagamati River, 17, 100
Bahadur Shah, 27
Balakrishna Sama, 40
Bangkok, Thailand, 59
Barter system, 72
Barzun, Jacques, 176
Basundhara, Prince, 67
Benares, India, 38
Bhadgaon, Nepal, 24, 25
Bhimphedi, Nepal, 43
Bhote Kosi River, 154, 155
Bhrikuti, Queen, 22, 23
Bhupatindra Malla, 25
Bhutan, 91
Biratnagar, Nepal, 73
Birendra, Crown Prince, 67, 173n.
Birkishore Pande, 32
Bir Shamsher, 40, 41
Bishop, Barry, 156
Bista, Colonel, 155, 160
Bodnath, Nepal, 18, 19–20, 24
Boster, Gene, 8
Botsford, Gardner, 7
Brahmans, 22, 34
Breitenbach, Jake, 133, 165
Britain and the British, 25, 27, 28–29,
    30, 33, 38, 40, 41, 44, 61, 92, 93,
    133, 136, 137–38
British Army, 25, 28, 29, 30–31, 78, 90
British Royal Air Force, 65
British Everest expedition (1953), 142

Bubonic plague, 75
Buddhists and Buddhism, 18, 21, 22–23,
    78, 79, 94, 163
Bulgaria, 92

Cabin, The, Kathmandu, 71
Calcutta University, 41
Camp, the, Kathmandu, 71–72
Canada, 92
Caronia, R.M.S., 59
Caste system in Nepal, 24, 39
Census, Nepal national, 72–73
Chandra Shamsher Rana, 39, 41, 42–43
Chawla, Ravi, 71–72
Chevalley, Gabriel, 141
China and the Chinese, 16, 22, 27, 40,
    44, 45, 47, 48, 78, 86, 89, 90, 91,
    93–95, 144, 151–52
Chini Lama, 19–20, 24
Chobar Gorge, 17, 23
Chou En-lai, 47n., 93
Churchill, Sir Winston S., 46
Cigarettes in Nepal, 70, 114
Climbing-permit fees, 135–36
Coapman, John, 68–69
Communists and Communism, 44, 45,
    48, 59
Constitution of 1959, 46–47
Cook & Son, Thomas, 59
Cultural frontier, 171–72
Cultural life in Nepal, 172–73
Currency in Nepal, 72

Dalai Lama, 19, 94, 132
Dashinkali, Nepal, 23
Dassain festival, 146, 153, 160

Democracy in Nepal, 46, 48–49

Democratic Innovations in Nepal (Joshi and Rose), 28, 44–45

Denman, E. L., 139

Deva Shamsher, 41

Dharmarkar, 16

Dhir Shamsher, 39, 40

Diaghilev, Sergei P., 60

Diseases in Nepal, communicable, 76–77

Dolalghat, Nepal, 145

Dooley Foundation, Tom, 75

Dorje, Ang, *124*, 149, 150, 152, 155, 162, 165

Doti, Nepal, 73

Drinking water in Nepal, 67, 77–78, 147

Dudh Kosi River, 153, 154

Earthquakes, 25

East India Company, 28, 29

Education in Nepal, 78–81, 88, 157

Election of May 27, 1959, 46–47

Electric power in Nepal, 73, 89, 91, 92

English College, Kathmandu, 43, 80

Entry visa, 143

Everest, Sir George, 136

Fish farms, 76

Food production in Nepal, 83–85, 86–87

Foreigners, exclusion of, 26, 41–42, 59

Foreign relations, Nepal's, 90–95

Forest lands in Nepal, 88–89

Forest Nationalization Act (1957), 89

Fort, Raymond, 8, 87–88

France, 92

Fürer-Haimendorf, Christoph von, 159, 163

Ganesh, 175

Gangeatic Sea, 17

Ganges River, 17

Gania (hashish), 70

Gautama Buddha, 18–19

Ghurka soldiers, 23, 25, 28, 29–31, 65, 66, 67, 78, 90

Girvana Jadha Bikram Shah, 29

Godavari, Nepal, 79

Goiter, 158

Gombu, Nawang, 133

Gorkha, Nepal, 25–26

Greuber, Father, 26–27

Gulatee, B. L., 136n.

Gupta dynasty, 22

Gurkha Brigade, 30

Gurungs, 21

Gyanendra, Prince, 45

Hagen, Tony, 90–91

Haletzki, Vladimir, 60

Harrer, Heinrich, 91

Hashish, 70

Hawley, Elizabeth Ann, 8

Haynin, Guy de, 142

Health services in Nepal, 73–78

Hillary, Sir Edmund, 91, 135, 140, 153, 154, 157, 158, 161

Himalaya, Prince, 67

Himalayan Club of Darjeeling, 133

Himalayan Journal, The (Gulatee), 136n.

Himalayan Sea, 16

Himalayas, the, 17, 26, 27, 59, 88, 93, 133, 134, 135, 136, 144, 147, 153, 158, 162, 173

Hindus and Hinduism, 21–22, 24, 79, 94, 159

Hippies in Kathmandu, 69–72
Hodgson, Sir Brian, 29–30
Hong Kong, 31
Hospitals in Nepal, 73
Hydroelectric power, *see* Electric power;
    Water power

India and the Indians, 17, 29, 30, 33, 42,
    44, 48, 57, 61, 78, 83, 89, 90, 91,
    92, 93–95, 144
Indian Army, 25, 57
Indian Congress Party, 61
Indian National Airways, 57
Indra, 167, 175
Indra Jatra festival, 175
Indrawatti River, 145
Industrialism in Nepal, 88–90
International air travel, 58–59
Irvine, Andrew, 138, 139
Israel, 92–93

Jaccoux, Claude, 135, 140, 141, 142, 143,
    144, 145, 146, 147, 148, 149, 150,
    153, 154, 163, 164, 165
Jaccoux, Michèle, *126, 128*, 135, 140,
    143, 144, 145, 146, 147, 148, 149,
    150, 151, 156, 160, 163
Jang Bahadur Kunwar, 31, 32–35, 36–41
Japan, 92, 136
Jawalakhel, Nepal, 91
Jiri, Nepal, 91
Joshi, Bhuwan, 28, 44
Journey to Kathmandu, A (Oliphant), 35
Juddah Shamsher, 44

Kala Pattar, 165
Kalden, Kapa, 163
Kali, 23
Karkotak, 15
Kathmandu, Nepal, 17, 23–24, 25, 26,
    29, 31, 42, 43, 45, 48, 49–50, 57,
    61, 62, 65, 67, 73, 80, 92, 95, *102,
    103*, 143, 175
Kathmandu Valley, 16–19, 21, 22, 23,
    24, 26, 36, 42, 62, 68, 72, 77, 80,
    85, 86, 137, 144
Kennedy, John F., 134
Kennion, Colonel, 30
Khampas, 94
Khumbu, Nepal, 68, *129*, 132, 158
Khumbu Glacier, 164, 165
Khumjung, Nepal, 154, 156, 159
Kipling, Rudyard, *quoted*, 11
Kirantis, 18, 21
Kirtopur, Nepal, 26
Kitchener, Lord, 42
Koirala, B. P., 47, 92
Kot Massacre (1843), 32–33
Kubrick, Stanley, 7–8

Laise, Carol, 8
Lakshmi Devi, Queen, 31–33, 37–38
Lambert, Raymond, 140, 141
Landon, Percival, 30, 33, 41–42
Landownership in Nepal, 43, 85
Land-reform program in Nepal, 85–87
Land Acts of 1957 and 1964, 85
Langtang, Nepal, 91
Languages in Nepal, 21, 72
Le Bon, Gustave, 50–51
Leeches, 141, 144, 148–49, 151, 153
Legal code of Nepal, 34
Lelyveld, Joseph, 174

Lévi, Sylvain, 41
Life expectancy in Nepal, 42, 78
Limbus, 21
Lissanevitch, Boris Nicolaevitch, 8, 59–66, 67
Lissanevitch, Inger Pheiffer, 62, 63
Lissanevitch, Kira Stcherbatcheva, 60, 62
Lukla, Nepal, 153
Lumbini, Nepal, 18

Magars, 21
Mahabir Shamsher Jang Bahadur Rana, General, 61, 62
Mahendra Bir Bikram Shah Deva, 18, 26, 40, 44, 46, 47, 48, 56, 62, 63, 67, 79, 80, 81, 92, 93, 94, 95, 174
Malaya, 31
Malla, Kamal P., 49
Malla dynasty, 24, 25, 26, 28, 173
Mallory, George Leigh-, 137–39, 140
Malaria control in Nepal, 75–76
Manjusti, Bodhisattva, 16, 17
Mao Tse-tung, 95
Maraini, Fosco, 171–72
Marbhupal Shah, 26
Massine, Léonide, 60
Matrimonial customs in Nepal, 24
McKinnon, John and Diane, 8, 154, 156, 157–60, 165
Medical services in Nepal, 73–78
Mineral resources in Nepal, 88–89
Missionaries, 26–27, 78
Mohan Shamsher, 44, 45
Monsoons, 89, 140–41, 144, 153, 158
Moran, Father Marshall, 78, 79
Mountain Travel, 134, 141, 153, 159, 165, 166
Mount Ama Dablam, 156

Mount Annapurna, *see* Annapurna range
Mount Cho-oyu, 135
Mount Dhaulagiri, 135, 137
Mount Everest, 17, 47n., 65, 68, 95, 122, 132, 133, 135, 136–42, 144, 149, 153, 154–55, 156, 157, 160, 161, 165
Mount Everest expeditions, 136–67
Mount Kanchenjunga, 135
Mount Lhotse, 135
Mount Makalu, 135
Mount Mansalu, 135
Mustang, principality of, 43, 94

Namche Bazar, Nepal, 127, 132, 139, 140, 146, 155, 158, 160, 163, 165
National Communicable Disease Center, Atlanta, Georgia, 74–75
National Panchayat, 48
Naura, Nepal, 73, 74, 75
Nehru, Jawaharlal, 44, 93
Nepal, 15–51, 72–96, 139, 143, 172, 176
Nepal (Landon), 30, 41–42
Nepalese Army, 32, 35n., 56, 92
Nepali Congress Party, 44, 45, 47, 93
Nepal National Museum, 37
Nepal Rastra (Central) Bank, 63, 87
Nesti, Nepal, 26
Newars, 21, 24–25, 64, 66, 145
New York Times, The, 174
New Zealand, 91, 157
Norkay, Tenzing, 135, 139, 140
Norton, E. F., 137, 138

Ochterlony, General, 29
Odell, N. E., 138–39

Odessa, Russia, 59, 60
Oliphant, Laurence, 28, 35, 36–37

Padma Shamsher, 44
Pagodas, 23–24, 25, 97
Pakistan, 92
Pan American Airways, 75
Panchayat system, 47–48, 88
Patan, Nepal, 24
Patna, India, 78
Peace Corps, U.S., 56, 81–83
Pema, Ang, 133
People's Party (Praja Parishad), 44
Pheriche, Nepal, 164
Pokhara, Nepal, 17, 58, 68, 143
Political parties in Nepal, 44, 45, 48,
    80, 93
Population density in Nepal, 77
Prajapati, 166
Prayer wheels, 20–21, 115
Prime ministers in Nepal, 27–28, 29, 30,
    31–32, 38, 40, 41, 43, 44, 45, 47
Prithi Vir Vikram Shah, 40
Prithwi Narayan Shah, 26, 27, 28

Races of Nepal, 21
Raiguru, the, 40
Railroad, 43
Rais, 21
Rajendra Bir Bikram Shah, 31–33, 37, 38
Rana, Sub-Inspector, 126, 155–56, 160,
    165
Rana dynasty, 27, 32, 33–50, 61, 72, 78,
    85
Rapti Valley, 76, 84
Ratna, Queen, 40

Religious attitudes in Nepal, 173–74
Revolution of 1951, 45, 78
Rinderpest, 75
Rising Nepal, The (newspaper), 49
Roads and highways, 43, 57, 63, 66, 73,
    94, 144–45
Roberts, James Owen Merion, 134–35,
    141–42, 143, 145, 150, 153
Rongbuk Glacier, 138
Rongbuk Valley, 137
Rose, Leo, 28, 44
Royal Hotel, Kathmandu, 63–64, 65, 69
Royal Nepal Academy, 40
Royal Nepal Airlines Corporation, 55,
    57–58, 68
Rug weaving, 91
Russia, 90; see also Communists

Sainju, Mohan Man, 87–88
St. Xavier's elementary school, 78–79
Sanad, the, 39
Sankhu, Nepal, 66
Sanskrit, 21
Sati, practice of, 34
Savings program for farmers, compul-
    sory, 87–88
Scott, Esther, 63, 66
Segauli, Treaty of (1816), 29
Sepoy Mutiny (1857), 30, 41
Serpent's Lake, 15–16
Seven Years in Tibet (Harrer), 91
Shah dynasty, 25–33, 37–38
Shamsher Rana, Field Marshal Kaiser,
    35n., 37
Shangri La pass, 164
Shawn, William, 7
Sherpas, 21, 73n., 90, 116, 117, 131–35,
    136, 138, 139, 147, 148, 149, 151–

152, 157, 158, 162, 163
Sherpas of Nepal, The (Fürer-Haimendorf), 159
Shipton, Eric, 140
Shoyambhu, the Self-Existent One, 15, 16
Sikhdar, Radhanath, 136
Sikhi Buddha, 16
Sikkim, 17, 91
Singh, General Abhiman, 32–33
Singh, Gagan, 32
Singh, General Mahatabar, 31–32, 37
Singha Durbar (palace), 42
Slavery in Nepal, 34
Smallpox, 76–77, 158
Smithsonian Institution, 166
Soaltee-Oberoi Hotel, 67–68, 69
Social progress in Nepal, 73–75
Solu, Nepal, 68, 132, 158
Somervell, T. H., 138
Srang Tsan Gam Po, King, 22
Strikes, labor, 44
Stupas, 18–19
Succession, law of, 39, 40
Summer Institute of Linguistics, 56
Sun Kosi River, 145
Sunwars, 21
Surendra Bikram Shah, 31–32, 37, 38
Swayambhunath shrine, 18, 20–22, 98, 101
Swiss Association for Technical Assistance, 56
Switzerland, 90–91

Thapathali, Treaty of (1854), 40
Tharus, 21
Those, Nepal, 151
"300" Club, Calcutta, 60–61
Thyangboche monastery, 20, *108,* 132, 160–62, 165
Tibetan Blue Restaurant, Kathmandu, 70–71
Tibet and the Tibetans, 17, 19, 21, 22, 25, 27, 40, 45, 57, 59, 89, 91–92, 94, 131, 136, 137, 139, 143, 145, 153, 159, 161, 164
Tibetan Sea, 16
Tiger shoot, 35–36
Tiger Tops Hotel, 68, 69, 76, 143
Tihar festival, 175
Tobacco, 70
Tourists and tourism in Nepal, 31, 58–59, 63, 66–67, 68–72, 81, 95
Trade agreements, 92
Transportation problems, 84
Trekking permits, 143–44, 155
Tribal groups in Nepal, 21
Tribhuvan, King, 40, 44–46, 57, 61, 78
Tribhuvan Air Port, Kathmandu, 56, 57, 67
Tribhuvan University, 43, 74, 80
Tsering, Ila, 131–34, 135, 144, 145, 148, 150–51, 152, 153, 155, 160, 161, 162, 164, 165
Tuberculosis, 77, 132, 158
Tucci, Giuseppe, 173–74

Taxes and taxation in Nepal, 43, 62
Technological progress in Nepal, 176
Telephone system in Nepal, 73
Terai, the, 17, 18, 28, 31, 35, 41, 45, 57, 61, 68, 69, 75, 84

United Nations, 59, 92
United Nations Mission in Nepal, 56
United States AID program, 56, 73, 74, 75, 76, 80, 83, 87, 90

United States Technical Co-operation
    Mission, 83
Upraity, Dr., 80, 81

Vaccination programs in Nepal, 75, 76–
    77
Victoria, Queen, 33, 37
Vipaswi Buddha, 15
Visambhu Buddha, 16
Vishnu, 38, 174

Wang Huen Tse, 22
Water power in Nepal, 88, 89
Waugh, Sir Andrew, 136
Weatherall, Mickey, 57

West Germans, 92
Where Four Worlds Meet (Maraini),
    171
Whittaker, James, 133
Wilson, Maurice, 139
World Food Program, 76
World Health Organization, 74, 75, 76
World War I, 30
World War II, 31, 39, 139
Wright, Daniel, 39

Yak and Yeti Restaurant, 64–65
Yaks, 162–63, 165
Yaksha Malla, 25
Younghusband, Sir Francis, 137
Yugoslavia, 92